With love & blessings
from The Ol Sea Hag
Gracie Strom

Amazing Gracie
and
The Sea Hag

Thorn and Ursula Bacon

Amazing Gracie
and
The Sea Hag

Thorn and Ursula Bacon

BestSeller Books Inc.
Wilsonville, Oregon

Special recognition to Lynn Moyers for his contributions to this book.

Copyright 2009 by Thorn and Ursula Bacon
All rights reserved
Printed in U.S.A.
Library of Congress Catalog Number 2008941924
ISBN 978-1-4276-2385-0

Cover design: Kim McLaughlin
Text design: Sheryl Mehary

BestSeller Books, Inc.
P.O. Box 922
Wilsonville, Oregon 97070

Dedication

To all of you who touched my life,
who brought me your gifts,
your talents and your love,
and who were always at my side
when I needed you.
Thank you so much.

— Gracie

Gracie Strom

A Wish From an Old Mariner

May your charted course be true,
And the Sea Gods smile on you;
May the storm clouds fade away,
And blue skies remain all day;
As you sail without strife,
Upon the seas of Life.

Pull up your pants, it's too late to save your shoes."

~ From Gracie's Bag of Tricks

Chapter I

Depoe Bay, a once sleepy, one-block fishing village perched above a stormy seawall facing Oregon's Pacific Ocean's long reach westward to where the sun sets – has been known to boast of having the world's smallest harbor. In the same breath, the small coastal town rightfully claims recognition for harboring the biggest heart from the Pacific to the Atlantic. It belongs to Gracie Strom, the happy-go-lucky whirlwind with the energy of a small tornado, the generosity of a saint, the sympathy of a room full of new mothers and a deep sense of gratitude to the people who trust her with their loyalty and their friendship.

She's been called many names – Depoe Bay's Fairy Godmother; Amazing Gracie, the Enduring Benefactor of the Unfortunate and Luckless; the Bottle-Playing Sea Hag, and her tiny coastal town's Personal Statue of Liberty with the Porch Light On.

Gracie is all of these. She has fed the hungry, sheltered the needy and with the magic and charm of her childlike spirit has dispensed her own brand of irresistible inspiration to all who cross her path. Without concern for the outcome, she descends into some hapless soul's shipwrecked life like a dervish in skirts, turns it around and brushes off thanks and gratitude because praise embarrasses her and makes her feel uncomfortable.

A free-wheeling spirit, a woman of boundless energy and trust in the goodness of life, Gracie has lent her hand and heart for making dreams come true in an ever widening circle of love and admiration, which has made her reputation and her restaurant, the Sea Hag a much talked-about subject from coast to coast.

How does a young woman with two daughters and a son build a legendary reputation in a remote town – no more than a wide spot in the road – where only 150 people made their home in 1963? The answer is a remarkable story and it is about a widow in her thirties and her young children who within five years, converted a risky undertaking, a run-of-the-mill restaurant into an attraction that lured thousands of people from all over the U.S. to return to the Sea Hag year after year.

Ask anyone who has spent any time in Depoe Bay if he has been to the Sea Hag and you'll see a face light up with a fond memory and a wide smile accompanying the energetic nodding "OH! Yes! Of course. I've been to the Sea Hag, and I met Gracie." The secret of Gracie Strom is as American as the tradition of trying. Hers is also a tribute to her generation which has been called "the Greatest" because it was composed of people who were hardy, sentimental, street-wise, had a sense of humor and possessed a built-in determination to get ahead. Never did they give a thought to backing down when troubles came along.

Come along and journey through the life of Gracie Strom and her Sea Hag – a heartwarming odyssey of life, laughter and the making of a legend.

❦

Gracie Arianna Sax was born in Bridgeport, Washington in the heart of apple growing country. Her father Alfred J. Sax, a World War I veteran, moved from Arkansas to the Beebe Orchard area in the 1920s, where he met and married Agnes Hancock on

July 27, 1926 in Okanogan. Gracie was one of six children — three boys and three girls. The family lived in Bridgeport and Chelan before moving to Peshastin in 1930 to ranch. Mr. Sax operated an orchard until 1974 when he moved to Cashmere, Washington. He lost his wife Agnes in 1983 and later married Anna Phipps on August 27, 1985, at Wenatchee and they continued to make their home in Cashmere.

Even as a young girl Gracie was strongly independent and effortlessly versatile. She was learning how to drive the family farm Jeep while the kids her age were experiencing a set of training wheels on their first bicycles. Gracie and her dad liked to drive around in the family Jeep but were also often seen tooling about in their rattly, old farm pickup — for the fun of it.

Even though Gracie grew up in the Great Depression the Sax family never felt the pinch millions of Americans experienced. Chickens scratched and screeched in the barn yard, cows grazed getting fat for the table, vegetables and berries from their garden and fruits from the family orchard all contributed to the Sax family being well fed. Agnes made cottage cheese, butter, cream and buttermilk for their own use and sold the rest door-to-door along with fresh eggs and chickens. Gracie thought this was all great fun.

Since the area's schools were too small to be accredited and her parents thought it important for her to have a Catholic education, Gracie and her older sister Elaine went to boarding school. They attended and later graduated from Holy Names Academy in Seattle. Because they were sisters, the two girls were allowed to share a private room rather than living in the dorm. This arrangement proved to be invaluable because Elaine would not snitch on her sister and tell the nuns about any of Gracie's escapades — some of which would have brought even the sturdiest nun to her knees outside of the chapel. Gracie and her next-door neighbor, Mary Clark, would often crawl out of the window of their room, dangle their legs from the ledge, smoking cigarettes while planning their future. When some years later Gracie revisited the school and noticed how narrow the ledge really was — four stories up — she realized how easily they could have fallen off.

Having developed an almost irresistible charm early in life, it didn't take Gracie long to make the Most-Popular-Girl list. The school benefited from the young girl's proficiency in driving, allowing her extra freedom from the regimental discipline of a Catholic boarding school. She was just as much at home behind the wheel of the nun's big Lincoln sedan, as she had been driving the apple orchard's truck. Gracie caught on that many of her rebellious acts, such as dropping cigarette butts from the balcony on the Sister's habits were ignored because of her expertise behind the wheel.

At the same time, Gracie received a different kind of attention and earned a less flattering round of applause. She had been caught picking at her teeth with her fork trying to dislodge a wayward piece of spinach that had gotten stuck in one of her front teeth. Noticing the social blunder and not mincing any words, one of nuns rose from her seat at the table and announced, "We're now going to have Grace Sax stand up and give us a lesson on how to clean your teeth with a fork."

Gracie was terribly embarrassed and felt like crawling under the table and staying there for the duration. Later in life, this episode became one of the many tales she tells on herself with her blue eyes awash in mirth and her dimples laughing at herself and at the world.

While in high school, Gracie had a boyfriend in the Navy and he used to visit her ever so often. During his brief stays they would sit in the parlor together, along with a nun, never alone. The nuns had taught the girls that French kissing was a sin and that they could get pregnant from a kiss. Needless to say, all the girls had "stiff upper lips."

The Academy's chaplain was Father William Tracy, an Irish priest who wrote the book *The Rabbi and I*. Father Tracy had a remarkable effect on Gracie's life, along with other priests: Father David Cullen, Father Charles Zack, and Father Mel Stead. She has said for many years that she wished the Pope could have met them. These men had a great sense of humor and encouraged young people to have fun and enjoy their religion. Then, as now, faith is an important part of Gracie's life.

Some time in 1946, when Gracie was about seventeen, she wrote her mother a letter reminding her of her upcoming high school graduation and describing that she and her best friend were going to embark on a cruise for seniors and juniors to Seabeck.

"Elaine, and I," she wrote, "are getting new print dresses. Elaine is a whiz at sewing and I have quite a bit of striped material so we are going to make us each a dress at Zula's. She has a fancy sewing machine that even makes buttonholes so we can use that. She even put buttonholes in a blouse of mine I made, which I wanted to wear to go downtown. A seamstress would have charged quite a bit so I was happy to have Elaine do it for me.

"Mom, I hope you get this letter before Mother's Day. You'll see why because Lorraine Cole wrote a poem that Sister says is a marvel. It's part of this letter.

"Love you, Gracie and Elaine,"

Dear mother, you are God's sweet gift sublime;
You healed my earliest heartache, always dried
My earliest tears. Not death, nor pain, nor time
Can from my searching eyes your dear love hide.
So closely did you hold me to your heart,
To quiet my poor foolish, childish fears,
That my untested soul seemed the fragile part
Of yours, made stronger by the gentle years.
Yours is a love so true, sincere, and pure;
That where e're my steps may turn ... terrain or foam :
That love doth follow; and I shall feel secure!
And when at last God calls you to His home,
I'll pray, with all my heart, someday to be
Again with you ... for all eternity.

Toward the end of her high school years in Seattle, Gracie first met Dick Strom briefly one afternoon in 1942. It was through one of her best friends, Mary Clark, with whom she'd palled around during high school, that she'd met the strikingly handsome Marine pilot. From skiing to shopping, the two high school girls did everything together, but Gracie had never known anything about her friend's brothers until they came to visit. The young men were Navy flyers; "Weekend Warriors" they were called, and were stationed on Whidbey Island. One of Mary's brothers, a Naval officer, stopped by to see his sister and brought along a buddy, namely handsome Dick Strom, a Marine combat pilot in the Pacific during World War II. But it was Mary's brother who chatted with Gracie – an adolescent girl wearing black stockings and a stiff midi blouse. The girls were beside themselves, hyperventilating around these older, mature servicemen.

"Honest to Pete," Gracie recalled, a far away look in her eyes, "I just couldn't believe our friend was related to one of these handsome dudes. And of course, they didn't pay one bit of attention to any of us others."

Two years later, after Gracie had completed her freshman and sophomore years at Washington State University, she accepted a job at the YMCA in Wenatchee. There she was, the secretary and only female, at the YMCA. However, having been the ping-pong champion of Holy Names, she competed with many of the male YMCA boarders and pilot trainees. These young men, soon to be full-fledged "Fly Boys," were made to practice playing ping-pong to improve their eye muscles by keeping the ball steady in their sight. The fast and furious exercise of zeroing in on the small white ball and sending it across the net, would train the fledgling pilots to hit their targets in bombing raids more accurately. This daily practice helped them develop keen, surefire eyesights.

It was in the bustling and busy atmosphere of the YMCA that Dick Strom walked into her life for the second time. He was just as good looking as she remembered, well mannered and so very eligible. This time, he noticed the pretty young woman; he fell for Gracie. Dark-haired, with a beautiful face, a lovely figure and the desire for romance etched invitingly on her face, she was the only female employed at the Y where thirty young men had rooms and fanciful notions about Gracie. She did have a "steady" at the time Dick first asked her for a date but he was hard to resist. And it wasn't long before she was head over heels in love with the lively, energetic young man.

Dick had come to Wenatchee after he was discharged from the military and finished his degree at Washington State University at Pullman. His professors had implored him to become a Rhodes Scholar, but candidates had to be interested in teaching to qualify and that was not Dick's goal in life. He wanted to be in the middle of life rather than occupy an ivory tower in academia. He preferred to try his hand in business world and for starters joined a large fruit company in Wenatchee as a salesman.

About a year after they met, Gracie and Dick– rather than face the cost and demands of a big wedding, and practical to the core – opted for a coffee pot full of cash and eloped. The young couple was married on July 27, 1949, the anniversary date of the marriage between her father and mother. The newlyweds spent some of their coffee pot money on a brief Canadian honeymoon before settling down. Gracie had never been happier in her life and was looking forward to a bright future.

Chapter 2

Still influenced by the familiar traditions of the thirties, Gracie expected to give up her new job as a receptionist for a physician in Wenatchee. She told Dick that she was going to quit for the full time pursuit of being a traditional at-home-wife, making her man happy, taking care of him and planning a family, Gracie was surprised when her new husband said, "No. It doesn't work that way. You should keep your job with the doctor."

That was when she learned from Dick about the hard times his family had suffered when his father died during the Great Depression from the complications of diabetes. Dick was born in the Seattle area into a fairly well-to-do family. Unfortunately, his father had literally committed suicide because as a diabetic he was insulin-dependent but refused to take the insulin prescribed for him. Dick was the oldest of four children – three boys and one girl – the latter was the youngest of the four. His father had been a successful stockbroker and provided a comfortable, privileged life style for his family. But with the father gone during the height of the Depression, life was hard. Dick's mother had to shop at the little corner grocery store that extended credit to the family in order to buy bread for her children.

Eventually, his mother Jessie, found a job as a social worker and life became easier for the Strom family. By then, Dick was a senior in high school and worked at odd jobs to supplement his mother's income. Somehow, like the rest of the country, the Stroms made it through the tough times.

Gracie felt blessed and lucky to be married to Dick. As a Marine pilot during the war, eager mothers had been trying their best to fix him up with their daughters left and right and had not been successful. In her mind she could never believe that she had been so lucky. He truly was Mr. Eligible and resembled the popular movie star, Montgomery Clift. He was a modest man with a great zest for life. He had time for everybody; he loved and respected older people, spent hours talking to them about their history, learning from them.

After they were married a short while, Dick, still in the Marine Corps Reserves, considered a proposition he received from Glen Yarborough of Limelighters fame. The two men were friends and Glen forecast a bright future for Aspen, Colorado as an upcoming ski resort and asked Dick to come in as a co-owner in the development of a whole block of property that held a shabby, rundown motel. Aspen, a small out-of-the-way mountain village was unknown in the late forties and the undertaking would be quite a gamble. It was several years before Aspen was discovered and became the popular and posh ski resort that attracted the wealthy, making real estate prices soar to heavenly heights.

Dick and Gracie turned down the offer. In the meantime, Dick had taken a job as assistant sales manager of Standard Fruit in Wenatchee where part of his work consisted of flying around the country and taking orders from fruit jobbers. His work took him to California, Arizona, Texas, Oklahoma, Arkansas, Alabama and Virginia. Needless to say, flying was a great bonus for him.

His transportation consisted of a single engine Luscomb, a light plane he had purchased for $1,500. Strangely enough, years later, his son Larry, just as fascinated and passionate about flying as his father, purchased the very same model for his first aircraft.

Wanting to stay involved and active in the world of aircraft, in June of 1950, flying solo, the former Marine pilot headed for maneuvers at Cherry Point Air Station in North Carolina to join the Air Reserve fighter squadron to stay on top of the latest methods of aerial warfare.

Prior to his engaging in the reserve military service, the young couple took advantage of his flying about the country for his fruit company by meeting at O'Hare Airfield in Chicago. They planned their secret getaways to coincide with Gracie's vacation from her job and had the best times.

"We always stayed at the Palmer House," she reminisced wistfully, her expressive eyes sparkling with the memory of good times. "In those days," Gracie continued, "there was a spot in front of the Palmer House where we could land our little airplane. It was a midway island, just a narrow strip of land. I would fly from Seattle to Chicago's O'Hare Airport where Dick had landed his small plane alongside one of those huge Boeings. I'd get off my big plane, climb into his little Luscomb and we'd take off for the short jump to downtown Chicago where Dick set down the plane on that tiny, slim sliver of land right outside our hotel. What fun! We'd spend a couple days, enjoying the luxury of that famous hotel and got lost in the hustle of big city life. We then headed for Utah and Colorado stopping at fruit brokerage communities so Dick could take care of his customers." Young, carefree and just starting out in life, Dick and Gracie had a grand time.

Fortunately, Dick was an excellent pilot and a lot of luck was on their side that day in Wyoming when they came face to face with danger. It was in the middle of summer on a beastly hot day when Dick had landed in Rock Springs to take on fuel. During takeoff, perhaps due to the high altitude, the small plane was unable to gain power for lift off. They had almost reached the end of the runway, when their luck held — they had just enough power to avoid plunging into a drop of about 10,000 feet.

"Oh, thank God, we made it," Dick had sighed audibly, letting out a deep breath. Relieved, he admitted to his young wife how closely they had flirted with death.

Not long after their last fling in Chicago, Dick was called back into the Marines. Gracie noticed the resentment Dick fought to hide about his recall to active duty. He was headed for Korea. A decorated hero of World War II, neither Dick, nor his new bride had been paying much attention to the growth in hostilities between North and South Korea. The boiling tension in this divided country – encouraged by the Soviet Union – was reported daily in the national news as it became more and more inevitable that the United States would have to support South Korea.

Dick's reserve status threatened the couple's future plans. But the rumors of war grew more decisive and two years later, Dick Strom was back in uniform. On leave from his job he and Gracie, the latter pregnant with their first child, set up house near El Toro Naval Air Station, where Dick was stationed.

The first signs of the arrival of the baby started about three o'clock in the morning of April 6, 1952. Dick hurriedly bundled Gracie into the car and took off for the hospital in Santa Ana. Feeling the pressure of imminent birth, the about-to-be mother kept telling her husband to stop the car. "Stop the car!" she yelled, "the baby's coming. The baby's coming!"

Barely in time and with lots of luck once again, they reached the hospital. Gracie was wearing shoes that laced up which she literally kicked off, ripped her smock off of her body, certain the baby was coming.

Dick fidgeted about nervously and finally announced that he had to get some cigarettes. He didn't admit it until later, confessing that he was having sympathetic labor pains.

"As soon as they had me in the delivery room," Gracie said, "this nurse took one look and shouted, 'Oh my God, that baby's coming!'" Right then, no more than five minutes later, and with help of a light anesthetic and a spinal, Nancy Strom entered the world. Gracie's doctor had not arrived in time for the event and it had been up to the nurse to deliver the baby. When Dick finally returned with his cigarettes, had settled himself into a chair in the "expecting" father's room and nervously started smoking, he was the father of a baby girl.

"I did have a real big-boobed nurse who was there to see me through the process," Gracie confessed.. "I was scared. I didn't know what to do — I'd never had anything to do with babies. None of us at home had ever babysat or had taken care of infants. But that big nurse was a practical woman. She just picked up that screaming, kicking baby and held her against her generous chest and that baby was just fine, just perfect."

Nancy was just a few weeks old when Dick and Gracie left her in the care of a motherly friend and took off for Catalina Island for short "honeymoon" just before he would have to leave. The young couple had a three-day vacation away from the baby and time for each other. Dick then left for Korea where he joined the same squadron in which he had served in World War II. All of the men had been called back. None of them liked it, but the pilots, like Dick, had their war mapped out for them. They would be able to resign their commission after the completion of their tour of duty in Korea. Dick hated Korea. During World War II, he and the others had been heroes, protecting their country and the freedom of mankind. But Korea was another story, Not that wars are popular, but after the Korean campaign the heroic men of countless death defying battles were forgotten.

Dick always felt that he killed women and children needlessly in Korea and carried a heavy load of guilt for the rest of his life. Most Americans encouraged to think of the Korean war as a "police action" did not realize the economic effect Army, Navy and Marine reservists ordered back to duty had on employers who were building businesses that had suffered just a few years earlier from the absence of men serving in World War II. Dick's boss and friend's appeal for Dick's release from Korean duty in 1953, was typical of many of the letters employers sent to the U.S. Marine Commandant who had the power to relieve World War II veterans from extended military service in Korea. Dick was aware of the letter and it gave him both a sense of appeal for personal justice and a slight sense of guilt, since he was intensely loyal to his country.

He had earned the Distinguished Flying Cross in World War II and later, a Gold Star in lieu of a Flying Cross for aerial attacks against the enemy in Korea. But he was refused relief from his service and stayed on until he completed a total of eighteen years of military reserve service. Gracie's young husband was a red-white-and-blue patriot who loved his country.

But he was grateful for the letter from Standard Fruit, for it expressed their high esteem for Dick as well as the loss of his contribution to the success of the company. The irony for Dick and Gracie was that he served in Korea for a little over one year and then was transferred to Florida for another year on nonessential stateside duty. That year in Florida seemed wasted. Gracie had joined him there and shared his frustration.

"We had nothing to do there. The officers, like Dick, were all captains and colonels by then. But we women couldn't get a job. We sat around the swimming pool and drank booze all day. A lot of the men flew around trying to overcome their boredom by being in the air. There was nothing for them to do except to serve the required time to be eligible to be discharged with a total of eighteen years in the Marine Corps Reserve.

"I remember thinking how the Naval Service bureaucracy was run by Washington dumbheads who didn't have the sense to get out of the rain when it came to caring for the lives of our nation's heroes."

Except for that year in Florida, Gracie lived at home with her folks on the farm until Dick returned. During that time the couple had saved some money and decided to invest in a business of their own. They placed an ad in the Wall Street Journal looking for a business opportunity that appealed to them. After much looking around, they invested in a company (Stackhouse Athletic Equipment), a manufacturer of stainless steel sports equipment and promptly lost their money.

Not long after that financial disaster, and still looking for a business, the Stroms came across an advertisment announcing the sale of a no-name restaurant in a no-name town. Undeterred and full of youthful bravery, they borrowed enough money from Dick's uncle and Gracie's dad to finance the acquisition of that small restaurant in a nondescript fishing village on the Central Oregon coast. With that purchase a whole new world was waiting for them and became the foundation for the "growing" of Gracie and the success she now shares with her family and friends.

Chapter 3

It was a blustering, stormy, wave-whipping day in February of 1963 when Gracie and Dick with their children, Nancy, Larry, and Sally, arrived in Depoe Bay – population 150 – as the new owners of The Sea Hag. The latter was a small, smoky restaurant and bar, rather listless and ordinary. People were served food on one side of the establishment, but in order to have a drink, they had to leave their table, go out the front door and enter the bar by its separate entrance.

Highway 101, also called the Pacific Coast Scenic Highway. ran past the front door of the Sea Hag. Though both Gracie and Dick had been raised in the Northwest – the Oregon coast was a wild feast for the eyes. They had driven to Portland from Seattle, then proceeded west on US Highway 26 to the cutoff that led to Seaside, Oregon. South was their destination, the sleepy fishing village of Depoe Bay, the Guinness record holder for having the smallest and most turbulent salt water harbor in the world.

In 1963, the Oregon coast, thick with trees that covered the coastal mountains like a velvet mantle of green was not heavily traveled. For miles of curving highway crowded with these fir and deciduous trees, the odometer on an auto would register 25 or 30 miles of lonely stretches without so much as the sign of a gas station or a single habitation. The only sounds were the wind driven rains assailing the coast with storms coming in from the Pacific and the crescendo of waves rushing in. The rain was not constant and breaks in the weather turned an afternoon suddenly beautiful and miraculously bright with sunshine.

Gracie and Dick stopped late in the afternoon to gaze at Cape Foulweather, the blustery headland frequently assaulted with wind gusts of 100 mph or more. Cape Foulweather was named by Captain James Cook in 1778. It was his first glimpse of land since leaving the Sandwich Islands. The sea was like a sheet of deep lapis that stretched all the way to the horizon. Gracie and Dick stopped at a scenic turnoff and marveled at the foam-capped waves that crashed against rocky outcroppings.

Fortunately for Oregonians and lovers of the coast, Oswald West, the state's governor from 1911 to 1915, decided to declare Oregon's beaches a public highway. The result of his foresighted-ness was that, despite some threats in the late 1960s, virtually all the coast became accessible to the public. A map of Oregon shows state park markings that dot the coastline like a string of pearls. These aren't the kind of state parks that you may expect. In many cases they are no more than a parking lot. But those parking lots as Dick and Gracie discovered, led to expansive beaches, tide pools and other natural beauties waiting to be explored.

Those parking lots provided another lesson in contrasts though. Most have signs warning: "Valuables Are Not Safe In Vehicle." Yet on this road the couple also found something they thought had disappeared along with kinder, gentler times – hitch-hikers. They didn't keep track but must have seen at least half a dozen individuals or couples trustingly standing or sitting by the side of the road with thumbs cocked.

People who live in Oregon and along its majestic coast revived Gracie's spirit. These were friendly people; helpful people. During Gracie's entire trip – from Portland to Depoe Bay, they didn't run into a single unfriendly person.

A wild and attractive small village was the Depoe Bay Gracie and Dick found in February 1963. Most startling and thrilling when they parked in front of the restaurant they had bought was the sudden crash of thunderous waves spending themselves against the sea wall just across the street. Most spectacular was the jetting stream of water that rose from the rocks below the sea wall in a thick stream of spray, as if shot from a pressure hose. The column of salt water climbed a hundred feet or more in the air, then came crashing down onto the highway running away across the asphalt and splashing sheets of ocean water against the doors and windows of the merchants' shops across the street, drenching the tourists strolling along the street.

It seemed to Gracie that the spouting horns were a boisterous greeting and she realized in an instant that it was a natural wonder people would love to come and see especially when the weather made the Pacific rough. She was also aware that the quaint village must be overflowing with seafaring history and ambiance, as it had captivated homesteaders and visitors alike for more than 70 years.

Depoe Bay was surrounded on three sides by forested hills and magnificent water-sculpted cliffs, and fronted by ancient volcanic rock formations often spewing 60-foot-tall geysers during high tide in the winter months. Gracie was soon to learn that it was the only town along the coast where sightseers could shop, dine, even visit a fine art gallery, have a picnic, watch a magnificent winter wave choreography, and sleep like a baby right next to the Pacific Ocean – which was kept at bay by nothing more than a solid old weathered stone seawall.

As if all this wasn't enough, Depoe Bay also sported what was purported to be the world's smallest navigable working harbor – and probably one of the most picturesque to boot at any season. When Gracie got up each morning before dawn (depending on the season and weather permitting), she watched boats heading out for whale watching or fishing. These small vessels could be seen negotiating the narrow, and sometimes treacherous, harbor opening leading under Depoe Bay's picturesque historic bridge. At sunset, they sailed silently back toward the harbor entrance, calling ahead to warn others away from the one-boat narrow channel passageway.

The day after arriving in Depoe Bay Gracie explored the end of an unusually well-marked pier – a part of the adventure for tourists where they had a chance to peek into fishing trawlers, sleek pleasure craft and whale-watching cruise boats.

Starting in December, she discovered hand-scrawled signs declaring "live crabs" nailed to telephone poles along the highway, with arrows directing newcomers down the winding Bay Street road, past the picturesque Coast Guard station, to the postcard perfect harbor. Visitors who chartered boats for bottom fishing came face to face with magnificent gray whales reported having had the experiences of a lifetime. Chances were good that Grays could be spotted year round along Depoe Bay's coastline – earning the town its title of "Whale Watching Capital of the World."

Charter whale watching and fishing trips were negotiable with any boat master who catered to the public. Depoe Bay's harbor was also home to a U.S. Coast Guard Search and Rescue Station that occupied the northeast corner. The "Coasties," as the residents fondly referred to the men who staffed the station, were on hand to come to the aid of a boat or individual in trouble in the often-treacherous water – and they were the town's pride and joy, Gracie learned.

Her busy mind went to work. It was clear to her after her tour of Depoe Bay that if she could lure the Coast Guard sailors and officers, the fishermen and the locals to her newly-acquired restaurant, she might be able to squeak through the stormy winter until summer visitors arrived at the scene.

Gracie and Dick Strom's new venture in the restaurant business – in a village of only one hundred and fifty people – got off to a slow start. It was in the middle of winter and not only was the tourist season still months away, but in 1963, the Oregon coast had not yet been discovered by the nation's vacationing fair-weather travelers. It would take time for the tide to turn.

Their Sea Hag would have to earn enough money to carry the Strom family of five, as well as their small staff, through the rough months. They would have to rely mainly on the income from the locals, and that included the "Coasties." The hosts of the Sea Hag welcomed the sailors and the fishermen to their restaurant and bar with a pleasant, comforting atmosphere, good food and drinks that were not expensive. The "boys" could run a tab that they settled on payday once a month.

Gracie turned out to be a natural hostess and her warm, personal greetings were an irresistible invitation for returning to the Sea Hag. Blue eyes sparkling, a genuine smile as wide as the ocean front and a firm handshake pulled the customer instantly into a world of caring. She treated everyone like an old friend renewing contact with people she hadn't seen for years.

Hands on her hips, a mischievous grin washing over her lively features, she'd holler her greeting: "Well! What took you so long to get here? We've been waiting for you!" Spying a customer on his way out the door, she would pop up at his side, place an arm around his shoulder, and bellow: "Who gave you permission to leave?"

At the same time Dick took care of customers by tending bar. His sparkling personality and witty ways added to the appeal of visiting the Sea Hag. However, Gracie realized from the start that they would need a gimmick, some unique attraction, something fun, to draw more and more people to their establishment, especially on those cold winter nights when the cozy home fires were beckoning. A short while before on a ride up the coast, she had watched a man behind the bar at a restaurant where she had stopped who had arranged a chorus line of liquor bottles which he "played" with a couple of sticks in time with a rock and roll number from the jukebox.

"Well," she thought, "I can do that! Maybe even better!"

With that in mind, she went to work and ended up creating her own boisterous, noisy and infectious, fun-breeding atmosphere. She learned to play different sounds on the array of liquor bottles displayed prominently against a big mirror behind the bar. Her instruments were unorthodox which only enhanced the charm of her performance. While Spike Jones blared from the juke box, Gracie's bar spoons danced across the row of liquor bottles, supported occasionally by the attention-getting sound of Dick's old Marine whistle (rescued earlier from his WW II F-4U fighter plane), the rich clanging of cowbells, the raucous honking of a car horn, and the teasing ripple of a kazoo.

Coming to the end of her energetic, well rehearsed perform-ance – a hell-bent-for-fun grin on her face – Gracie turned her backside halfway to her audience and with a noisy wooden rattle smacked her bump-and-grinding rear end all the way to the very last note. Her face flushed with pleasure, she bowed to the thun-derous applause of her guests.

A few feet away from the bar was a circular fireplace centered in the twilight room surrounded by chairs and tables where patrons were served cocktails with a full view of Gracie making her music. Firelight gleamed on bottles of Jim Beam and Bailey's Irish Cream and dozens of other popular brands. When a customer rose to leave during her performance, Gracie zeroed in on that individual and laughingly hollered, "Don't leave or I'll get depressed."

Not a day would go by without several people eagerly asking, "Is Gracie playing the bottles? Is she going to play again?" And play, she did.

While outside neon signs and flashing lights announced: Gracie's Sea Hag, Food and Grog, the interior of the restaurant was gradually remodeled over the years to resemble the captain's quarters on a large ship. The stained wood paneling and flickering oil lamps mounted on the wall created a relaxed softly lighted atmosphere, and gave character to the environment in which the restaurant is set. The walls were covered in fishing paraphernalia of the past and present, including a photograph of a girl holding an eel as long as her slight body.

Another photo showed a young man behind a huge scale surrounded by hundreds of fresh fish to be weighed for shipment. A Restaurant and Hospitality Award attested to the merit of the cuisine's praiseworthy quality. At the back of the restaurant glass-encased photos displayed captains and skippers of trawlers, with their holds full of fish from the Pacific Ocean which was less than a block away across the street.

The fact that the fish for the Sea Hag's tables made their way into Gracie's kitchen straight from the sea prompted her to announce: "Our fish is so fresh the ocean hasn't missed them yet." Now, more than five decades later, Gracie's words are still the slogan that carries the message of quality to the restaurant's patrons.

After Gracie and Dick had invested all the money they could raise to buy the Sea Hag finances were tighter than tight. During those lean years when a bar customer asked for a drink that wasn't stocked in the bar, Gracie would explain cheerfully, "Dick'll fix it for you in just a moment. I'll have to go to the stockroom to get your brand."

She skipped out, yanked a five-dollar bill from the restaurant cash register and hustled two doors down the street to the State Liquor Store and bought the particular bottle of booze the customer had requested. Back at the bar within three minutes, she handed Dick the bottle reminding him of the name of the drink for which the patient customer had asked. Generally the price charged for the drink covered about thirty percent of the cash Gracie had paid out for the bottle.

Gracie's talent making music on the liquor bottles was not a result of the piano lessons she had taken for six years when she was a girl and her plunking had been the worst kind of punishment her mom could have dreamed up for her and her sister. By the time she was a young adult she had developed a natural gift to push the boundaries within which she worked. And as much as she hated running scales on the piano keys when she was a girl, she enjoyed the giant spotlight that centered on her bottle-playing musical renditions.

If the Sea Hag was to become a popular place for people to stop, she had to make an expressive and lasting connection with every patron who came to eat or drink. Gracie wanted freedom without appearing foolish. She believed that nothing was easier than to follow the natural flow where her journey of life took her. This meant that she could be her genuine self and she discovered with slight amazement but with no sense of achievement that people responded to her warmth and caring. Nothing, she concluded, was more fun than doing the unpredictable with someone to cement a friendship upon first contact. That was her personality and with her bottles, laughing eyes and generosity, she demonstrated the chance and oddity in music to make sounds that stood out. She reveled in the amount of noise she could make happen in four minutes – taking people out of themselves by joining with them in a new, different expression of something old and familiar. Life was all music and she danced to its beat.

This same freedom she allowed herself, she gave to her children by handing them the opportunity to be themselves. She gave them free rein to make their mistakes, to discover who they were and, in the end, to reinvent themselves. She watched them with a loving eye go through the ordeal of growing up, accompanied them roaming the globe from her place at the Sea Hag, snickered quietly at their escapades, and vicariously participated in every one of their adventures. Without judging, without criticism but with a heart of love, she gave her children room to iron out the kinks in their lives and now, can proudly look at three successful, caring individuals who adore their mother.

❧

The first cook Gracie hired for the Sea Hag was Nellie Munson who ran the kitchen until she died in 1980. Nellie was a "pseudo-grandmother" to five year-old Sally Strom, who worshiped the kindly woman with a generous chest. She loved to bury her head in Nellie's cushiony bosom and feel that she was surrounded with a comforting joy that erased every concern or uncertainty a little girl ever had. Nellie also kept her sights on Nancy and Larry, who from day-one – from the time they could reach the sink – had worked at the Sea Hag washing dishes, cleaning up and hanging around. The Sea Hag and Nellie's kitchen were the real home for the Strom children, who only went "home" to sleep.

Gracie learned quickly that Nellie Munson was an original woman who could cook up a storm and laugh at the mistakes in life. In time, Gracie learned all about her new chef whose family, after they left the old country, lived several years on an island in the Columbia River. "After marrying my husband, Everett, we moved to Depoe Bay," Nellie related one day. "At that time folks used to drive through town in back of the Coast Guard station here. Engineers had just started to build the first half of the bridge on Highway 101," she said.

In those days, the hub of activity in town was in the general store owned by Mrs. Ferguson. People would gather there to buy groceries, gasoline, pick up their mail, but mostly just chat. And there was a busy little hamburger joint at a spot by the bridge that used to serve home-style meals at a small counter. Hamburgers were 15 cents apiece.

"My husband's step-father and a friend of his started bringing the first tourists to the area by running passenger buses," Nellie recalled. "Slowly, over the years," she continued reminiscing," the bay began filling with boats – at first the Wisniewski family was the only one who fished commercially.

"I remember Father's first boat, the *Orphan Annie*, taking tourists fishing," she chuckled. "It was a clumsy, awkward boat, but his second one, the *Pauline B* was even more of a disaster. The boat had a glass bottom and each time my father would load up Sunday fishermen, they would take one look through the bottom and immediately be sick."

The story that remained clearest in her mind was the one she told Gracie about the last rum boat to hit the coast. At that time the Munson's were living at Whale Cove. "Rum runners," Nellie explained, "during the days of prohibition would bring in a load of whiskey from Canada to Whale Cove and bury it in the sand. As the tide rolled in, the evidence was covered.

"After each run, the rum runners would dig up what they had hidden before and pull it up on ropes by hand to higher ground. Trucks would be waiting to haul it to Portland and Vancouver. None of the local residents realized what was going on until the rum runners were caught in the winter of 1930–31. On its last run the boat, loaded with whiskey, hit the rocks close to the beach during bad weather. They tried to patch the boat, but to no avail. At eight o'clock in the morning the law swooped down on them and hauled about 750 cases of whiskey to the county seat at Toledo.

"A week later the culprits broke into the jail and stole back their own whiskey," Nellie laughed. "Two of the trucks were caught by the police but a third one got away.

"I was pretty young at the time," she mused, "and a little scared when word leaked out of what had been happening right on the beach where we lived. No more smuggling was reported and our little town relaxed. Later, when I was older, I took what I learned about cooking from my mom and stayed with it for a whole lot of years."

Though Nellie didn't have a recipe box, she had terrific memory. She never forgot a recipe once learned, and, coupled with an unerring "feel" for good cooking, for blending ingredients and quantities, she was a chef in her own right. Next to Gracie, she held up the roof at the Sea Hag. She was a kind and caring soul; who had found a family of three children, whom she took under her wings – her grandmother wings.

But there was another side to this beloved "grandmother." A big-boned, strong Scandinavian, feisty and self reliant, she had a volatile relationship with her husband, Everett ("Butch"), an okay guy when he was sober, but a mean and nasty drunk. Many were the nights when he came home, stewed to the gills and beat up on her. As a result, Nellie would lock herself in at the Sea Hag to avoid another unpleasant confrontation.

But then came the day when Nellie had enough. No! No more abuse from Butch. Her booze-guzzling husband had shown up at the Sea Hag earlier in the evening brandishing a gun, telling Nellie, "You better go home or I'm gonna shoot Gracie." Nellie went home all right.

She waited up for him to arrive home stewed to the gills – all prepared. She didn't have to wait long. There came the early morning hours when Butch rolled in roaring drunk, yelling at the top of his voice. As soon as he stepped into his house, Nellie hit him squarely on the head with her favorite, heavy, black cast iron skillet – not once, but three times. Butch hit the floor like a puppet whose strings had been cut. She left him where he'd dropped.

When he woke up after hours of sobering sleep, he asked his wife what had happened. Nellie told him what she had done to him and informed him if he ever threatened her again she would repeat the iron-skillet revenge. She must have made her point; he never laid a hand on her again.

Nellie died in May 1980, just days before Mt. St. Helens erupted. Butch had passed away some years before. Nellie told many folks at the Sea Hag that when they put her in the ground beside Butch, that's when the mountain would blow. She was pretty close.

❧

Gracie's built-in attitude of familiarity brought customers back again and again

It was Gracie who became the heart of the Sea Hag. It was Gracie and her kids working every job at the restaurant that made the difference in the early years between survival and failure. There were many months when a profit of $250 after expenses was an amount to celebrate. Sally only five years old at the time stood on a stool at the kitchen sink to wash dishes. Her memories of those days are recollections of amusement at some of Gracie's antics, a deep appreciation of her mother's charity, an accusation she would have denied, saying "Helping folks who need a hand is just being friendly."

Today, Sally Strom, mother of daughter Tessa, son Austin and a granddaughter named Bella, is an accomplished artist, video producer and recent Master of Fine Arts. She wistfully recalls "Life with Mother." Sitting cross-legged on the floor, her long, shiny blond hair swept out of her face, her blue eyes sparkling just like Gracie's, she painted a colorful picture of the long-ago yesterdays.

She recalled the countless times when Gracie hired people off of the street, bought them clothes, got them settled in a place to live, and went out of her way to get them jobs when she couldn't hire them. The Sea Hag's innkeeper helped the less fortunate who crossed her path to start a new life. She never turned down anybody.

People would walk into the restaurant without the money to pay for just a handful of crackers – something Gracie picked up on instinctively. Soon a bowl of hot chowder appeared in front of the newcomers, and with a welcoming smile as bright as a summer day, Gracie sat down across from them and patiently listened to their stories, and without fail, gave them a hand up in her usual fashion.

And then there is other side of Gracie – the tireless, savvy and inventive entrepreneur. Sally fully believes that Gracie and her friend Stan Allan made Depoe Bay what it is today by creating a unique and appealing atmosphere for the little town. When Stan Allan established Trade Winds Charters, he started the sport fishing business in Depoe Bay, Gracie got busy and offered entertainment at the Sea Hag. Word got around. The crowds came to Depoe Bay to fish and happily ended up at Gracie's place. They relaxed with a "tall-one," told an equally tall fisherman's tale about The One Who Got Away, and with great gusto, helped themselves to generous portions of Nellie's good cooking.

The world is full of all kinds of people – an observation to which Gracie heartily agrees. After all, she has met them all across a bowl of steaming clam chowder or that "tall one." Among the many who made the Sea Hag their second home, was an elderly man who, like clockwork, came in every Friday night accompanied by his wife. They had a few drinks, ate their dinner and kept up lively conversations with other regulars.

When she died, a casualty of Alzheimer's, he eventually remarried, but his new wife – for some unexplained reason – stayed away. That did not stop him from making his regular Friday visits. He told Sally, "I go to church to see my acquaintances, but I come to the Sea Hag to be with my friends." His words fully explained why so many people who worked for Gracie stayed on for years. The Sea Hag was more like their families than their families at home.

Sally shifted her body, leaned against a huge leather hassock and turned the clock back some more. She explained that the restaurant was really "Home." Years later, when Gracie's children spread their wings and traveled the globe, staying away for months at a time, upon returning to Depoe Bay, headed straight for the Sea Hag. They never went "home." The Strom kids had a surrogate family. The restaurant's employees were their second Mom, Grandmother, Aunts and Cousins. The adopted head of the family was, of course, Nellie Munson, the cook who was the picture of a "typical" Mother, the Ladies-Home-Journal-Kind-of a Mother.

The Sea Hag was where the three Strom kids had their meals. Nancy complimented Nellie by saying, "Oh, we're going to be with somebody who knows how to cook." The fact was, the kids just stuck their heads in the kitchen and yelled, "Can we have half a grilled cheese and half a tuna sandwich?" Nellie filled the orders with love and added hugs and a special cuddling moment for Sally, the youngest.

Sally remembered details from the early years that were not only pleasant to recall but formed unforgettable recollections that created the mosaic of her life. She was surrounded by a reliable sense of family loyalty and sturdiness but was encouraged to develop an individual independence that became part of the solid core of her character. And then there were moments in her young life which years later still ring lightheartedly and send ripples of laughter into the grown-up Sally.

When the kids were in high school, their biology teacher confessed that as a young boy growing up in Depoe Bay, his mother would never allow him to walk on the same side of the street where the Sea Hag was located. Long before the Stroms ever bought the restaurant, it often was the place where some bottle-flying, chair-tossing and table-crashing fights came alive. They were noisy, body-bruising fights where customers and bar stools came flying out the door any time of the day or night; too bad if an innocent pedestrian got in the way of a fight-propelled object. So the young fellow's mother forbade him to walk on that side of the street. The broiling atmosphere at the Sea Hag has long since simmered down, but even with Gracie playing the bottles and an atmosphere of family and fun, there were occasional brawls in the bar. But that's the bar business.

Sally was quiet for a moment; her eyes half closed, she ventured far back into memorable childhood moments – unforgettable ones that never leave the recesses of our hearts and minds. She held dear the time when on Tuesdays after the school bus dropped her off at the Sea Hag (closed for the day) she and her dad always sat in the bar. Sally would drink colored water and he'd drink his booze. Father and daughter would look out of the window at the ocean and the sky and make faces out of the changing formations of clouds sailing high above their heads.. Day dreaming with him was fun and drew her closer to him. Even then she knew with a young girl's prescience that he was deeply troubled and alcohol washed over the memories that robbed him of his peace.

The Sea Hag was a demanding witch and hard taskmaster. The whole family spent most of the days – everyday – serving the restaurant, doing all but the cooking till the wee hours in the morning, only to start all over again long before sunrise. Holidays, vacations, leisure days or travel were at the very bottom of the must-do list. So Dick's decision one day to take the family to Los Angeles was greeted with shouts of joy.

Dick loved baseball and was a passionate Dodgers fan. Wild horses couldn't have kept him from driving to Los Angeles in 1963 to watch his beloved team play in the World Series. The Strom family piled into the car and drove to California. To Dick's delight – cheering and yelling – his dream came true; his favorite team won the coveted World Series, which made the trip a huge success. Arriving back in Depoe Bay, the World Series celebration took on a new meaning. The folks there were crazy about sports and went all out to voice their pleasure of the outcome of the "Big Game."

Friends and helpers had pasted huge Dodgers signs all over the Sea Hag, and every one of the windows of the restaurant was covered with a poster congratulating the Dodgers on their long awaited World Series victory. Thundering toasts and cheers rang out from the Sea Hag's bar, boiled over into the street, sailed over the sea wall and were swallowed up by waves. That night Gracie kept the bar open past three o'clock in the morning.

There were, of course the legal closing hours, but since the bar regularly shut down at two-thirty in the morning and the restaurant opened half an hour later at three, there wasn't much of a time gap.

During those days, Nancy and Sally then in their teens, were jokingly known as the "Sin Sisters." They were quite the drinkers and party creatures, not to mention all that other stuff that went on. In spite of all the partying, the girls never let up on their responsibilities. As soon as the last stay-to-the-bitter-end bar patron had left the establishment at closing time, the two Strom girls cleaned up at the bar while the employees switched over to work in the restaurant. When Sally was twenty-one she worked in the bar earning good money. She and Nancy would stay on after work and get smashed, consuming a small river of champagne until the restaurant crew got mad at them and tossed them out. Larry and his buddies would come to the Sea Hag before the school bus came and fix breakfast for themselves. Full of good food, they would clean the bar and in order to supplement the income they made in tips, they cleaned fish for the tourist fishermen who brought in their catch on charter boats.

There was never a dull moment as life at the Sea Hag went from one extreme to the other with the greatest of ease. No one raised an eyebrow when the news that Mondays were Bible study days at the Sea Hag reached the townspeople's ears. Without concern, without a thought of what the "neighbors" might think and without blinking an eye, Gracie invited the Bible study group to use the bar for their weekly discussion sessions. Dennis, who owned the gas station in the village, was the group leader and he and his six faithful happily showed up at the Sea Hag before the bar opened. The Strom girls swore to this day that the group was praying for them and their place in heaven. Unique and different in so many ways, the Sea Hag was the one place were people could come and talk about religion, about politics, the economy and any other controversial subject without causing a riot.

Never having been a place for much brawling, the Sea Hag is an orderly bar now. Gracie observes, "People don't drink a lot in our bar any more. They come because of the social contacts they make, the friends they meet and the pleasant atmosphere in the dining room." What Gracie in her modest ways didn't acknowledge was the fact that her presence, her warm and genuine appreciation of people, contributed to the comfortable ambience that stifled conflicts before they could get started.

Becoming a popular place, the Sea Hag had attracted a good number of local regulars and a set of tourist who never missed going to their favorite restaurant when visiting or going through Depoe Bay. But there was one time in the seventies, when Gracie noticed business falling off; no one was coming into the bar. She could not figure out what was going on. Puzzled, she opened the door and stepped out on the sidewalk, looking up and down "Main Street" (Highway 101). Then her eyes fell on a state police car parked across from the Sea Hag apparently watching the place and everyone who exited. With the force of being shot out of a cannon, a furious Gracie boiled across the highway to the trooper's car. In no uncertain terms, she told the policeman – whom she recognized to be a Sea Hag customer – to get his butt out of there, he was ruining her business. A firecracker discussion ensued between the two, with the end result of the trooper leaving the scene and a pleased Gracie watching business picking up again.

The Sea Hag attracted all kinds of patrons – dead and alive – and served them all well.

Sally recounts an unusual event that demonstrates the power of the Sea Hag community. Sally was working in the bar on a Friday night when young a widow arrived at the restaurant with the ashes of the departed and the whole grieving funeral party in tow. Her husband had asked her to "party" at the Sea Hag after his passing and his family and friends outdid themselves to honor his last request. The mourners danced with his ashes; they kissed the box and set it on Michael's piano. They drank to his life, they drank to his dying – and not too little of that. Sally said she thought the dear departed had the best time and she even felt teary-eyed with love for him, ashes and all.

As it was with so many small Mom and Pop enterprises, the budget for running the newly acquired restaurant was slim – if existing at all. There was no room for extras, not even a dishwasher. That problem was solved quickly when five-year-old Sally started working at the Sea Hag. Since hanging around Nellie the cook was her favorite past time and the little girl loved being busy, washing dishes turned from play to work. With her feet planted solidly on a big gallon tub in front of the sink, chatting away with Nellie, she washed dishes for hours at a time. Since the business was a family affair, after school, on weekends and on holidays, Nancy and Larry did their share of dish washing as well as waiting tables and being active members of the cleaning crew.

Gracie looked with pride on her children, pleased with their endless efforts to make a go of the struggling business. She treated her growing children the same way she treated life – she simply let "them" happen. Throughout the years into adulthood, she let them be, to taste whatever came their way, right or wrong. She exercised restraint in criticism. "How can you explain the idea of "hot" to children?" she mused. "They won't understand that until they burn themselves. Then, they understand: "hot."

Through thick and thin, through heartbreak and disappointments, through wrong choices and painful mistakes, Gracie's faith in a happy ending for her children never wavered. She stood at their sides with an open mind and open heart. She listened to their pain, she helped where she could and looked away when nothing else would do. And, it worked.

The same laissez faire approach to life spilled over into all her actions. Well, that's Gracie! Her hiring policy was just about as unorthodox as a pingpong ball at a tennis match. She hired strangers off the street who happened to ramble through town and had no place to go or a plan to get there – no references, no resume required. That hungry look, that lost and lonely shadow in their eyes was enough for the owner of the Sea Hag to hire the needy. But work at the restaurant was demanding. Those long hours on their feet, the push and rush at meal time, keeping track of who got the chowder and who got the eggs, was more stress than some helpers could handle; they didn't last long and left. But there was always an exception or two.

One who blew in with the ocean breeze and stayed on was Amber Morris, who tells the story of how she came to work at the Sea Hag. "It was a blue Indian summer day in September 1970," she recalled, "when my husband and I were driving up the coast.

The only reason we stopped in Depoe Bay was because we had a flat tire in front of Bob Jackson's grocery store. I looked around and on a whim crossed the Highway 101 to the Sea Hag. The moment I walked through the door, I met Gracie. I asked for a job and she not only hired me on the spot but offered to drive me to and from work daily. I was immediately captivated by this amazing, outgoing woman with the sparkling blue eyes. "Much later Nellie the cook told me that before her husband's death, Gracie was an introverted, quiet Catholic girl. But with Dick gone, the "real Gracie" emerged – her vivacious, people-loving self. (Thank goodness she didn't have twelve kids to rise like her sister.)

Gracie confessed that Amber was the first Hippie she'd met – a fact which made no difference. The Sea Hag's gracious hostess accepted the newcomer with open arms and put her to work in what was then called the "Poop Deck Room."

Another "steady" was a young woman, Jody Sax, who had just returned to the Depoe Bay area from Eugene and was looking for work. Jody's parents told her that she just had to visit the Sea Hag and meet the cute couple who was running the place. Her mother assured her that, "she'll just love the lady who's so sweet and so naive and reminds everyone of Gracie Allen."

To this day, Jody insists that Gracie hired her because they had the same last name – Sax. When Jody had first entered the Sea Hag, Gracie had come rushing up to her to check her out: "I thought you might be one of my long-lost cousins," Gracie laughed.

Short of operating monies translated into short of help. Often no more than two servers had to take care of the crowds. During the summer season, Gracie hired temporary help who had never worked in a restaurant and had no idea how to cope with a horde of hungry people. When hired help goofed or got drunk on the job, Gracie fired them on the spot. But when they came back the next day, full of apologies and tears begging for a second chance, promising never to sneak drinks again, soft-hearted Gracie rehired them back. On the other hand, some of those "temporaries" have been with her for decades – like Barbara Mason who has been a steady part of Gracie's life for nearly forty years.

Amazingly enough – through all the ups and downs – the business prospered, all because Gracie was the hub of the wheel and the loving, irresistible spirit of the enterprise. Her daughters insist that she was a feminist before the word was coined and has remained unaware of it. She was a feminist by circumstance, not by choice.

One of her grandchildren recently accurately characterized her in the way of an inner knowing that kids have and adults have long forgotten. Nancy's young son, Remington, expressed how much he loved his grandma, then said with a smile hovering in his eyes, "I saw a cartoon on television the other day that reminded me of Grandma. There were these two mice that had landed into a bucket of cream. One of the mice drowned, but the other mouse kept swimming. It was paddling around in a circle – round and round, again and again – until the cream had turned into butter and the mouse climbed out and walked away."

His favorite expression was one that had popped out of his grandmother's mouth one day when she had solved a nasty problem. "Just remember if the water's rising, pull up your pants, it's too late to save your shoes." She's only been doing it all her life.

Gracie is a survivor and her children learned the craft of surviving from her. There were tough times in her life other people may not have conquered, but she did. Her sense of equanimity is all encompassing and always came to her aide when she faced nuisances, lean times, disappointments, the death of four men in her life who were so dear to her and that sense of hopelessness that follows when things turn bad and threaten not to get better. Life was not a bowl of cherries; small things and big ones happened that could either defeat or inspire. In that case pondering the possibilities, Gracie opted to take a quick detour, knowing that it would lead right back to the road she had chosen to travel.

In spite of the countless daily chores, the long hours, the challenges and difficulties that were the scene from sunrise to sunset, Gracie and her children spent more time laughing than worrying about the uncertainty of the Sea Hag's future. Fortunately, there was also a light side to the story. Since the real essence of life was not about events, but about people, there was an endless parade of colorful, whacky and unique characters who crossed the threshold of the Sea Hag and lightened the load with their presence.

Gracie would never forgot the cold blustery night of 1967 when, "It was just getting dark, when I left the kitchen to unlock the door to the bar," she recalled. "Well, I didn't need the key to the door, because a bunch of our patrons had taken off with the door and the wind was blowing sheets of rain into the bar through the big hole in the wall."

Since Gracie had the bad habit of frequently running late opening the bar at the appointed time, her friendly public had taken a hand in teaching their favorite innkeeper a lesson.

A big grin dimpled her face and her eyes laughed as she continued. "We had to put up a temporary wooden barrier until we could find our front door."

Later that night she discovered that three of her best customers had stolen the door and abducted it. The door could be ransomed for six beers apiece. The culprits, Dick Braeche, Paul De Belloy and their pal, Jourgenson, had secretly planned the caper by oiling the door's rusty hinges for weeks so they could get it off easily when the time came for abducting the offensive barrier to good times. Between laughter and chuckles and a lot of back-slapping, the men had told her the door was so squeaky it was interfering with their drinking. Gracie had thought that oiling the hinges of the heavy door had been an act of kindness. She had no idea what was going on.

The abducted door was quickly located — including a ransom note demanding eighteen bottles of beer. The thieves had hidden that big chunk of oak at the old Boiler Bay Tavern. However, the guilty trio let Gracie know they wouldn't return the door until she had delivered the beer.

The Sea Hag's frontrunner was a good sport about the ransom and the thieves had had their fun. And, the fishermen quit hanging their handmade *Occasionally* sign over the *Bartender on Duty* plaque. "However," Gracie sighed, "they walked away with my sign that announced in bold letters: Bigger and Better Fish Are

Caught Here Than In The Ocean. I wish I had that sign now, because you know," she added, "it's probably true."

⚬⚭⚬

Then there was the time when one of her regular waitresses didn't show up for work. Quickly thinking of a replacement Gracie jumped in her car and drove to the house of Bonnie, who was enjoying a day off. Gracie charged in the front door yelling Bonnie's name and like an invading Swat Team searched for her from room to room. When she opened the bathroom door, she heard the shower running. That didn't stop her. She plunged right in and pushed back the curtain behind which, Bonnie, naked as the day she was born, had soaped her body and was shampooing her hair.

"Bonnie I need you at the Sea Hag right now," Gracie demanded. "I'm short a waitress and you're the first one that came to mind."

"Gracie, you're crazy. Can't you see I'm all wet, and there's nobody to take care of my son. I can't leave him alone," she protested.

"You dry off, I'll take Chris to my house; he'll be fine," she bargained.

Gracie, determined to get her way, wouldn't take no for an answer. She found Chris playing with his crayons and said, "Okay, Chris, come with me. We're going to my house. Your mom's got to work. Bring your crayons with you."

She and the boy were gone before Bonnie had toweled herself dry, and fluffed her wet hair. Twenty minutes later, she was at the Sea Hag waiting on customers.

It was just about an hour later when Gracie boiled into the restaurant holding Chris 's hand. "I'll take over your job and I won't baby sit Chris again. He scrawled figures all over my bedroom wall with his crayons while I was in the kitchen."

Bonnie took her son home. The next day when she reported to work, Gracie apologized for her abrupt manner, "I'm sorry Bonnie. It was my fault that I didn't watch Chris closer."

Bonnie just laughed. She loved Gracie for her caring and for her impetuous decisions. Her career at the Sea Hag lasted more than 40 years.

Gracie demonstrated shrewd business savvy when she and Dick drove to the Surf Point Inn to drum up customers. North on Highway 101, the Surf Point, poised about 150 feet above the ocean on a rocky promontory, was a glamorous bar, bordello and lodge for party-goers who came from Portland to be entertained by the beautiful girls whose favors could be acquired for drinks and a fee. The price was negotiable if the gentlemen required the attention of a companion for the night. The owners had invested heavily to install the fancy bar that revolved slowly in a circle. Customers clinging to drinks at the bar could turn slightly and watch the sun sink into the sea with a blaze of misty glory or with a last, lingering glow that spread along the horizon like a slow-burning fire.

However, not always was the weather mild and the ocean breezes gentle. There were the nights when storm winds smashed against the thick windows – twice with such a powerful force that hurled big logs through the glass with a devastating blow and a shrieking roar of storm fury. The water-soaked logs flew through the windows as though they were chopsticks, followed by a thunderous crash of glass, metal, and rough bark and landed on the carpeted floor, causing enough damage and danger to patrons that the lodge was shut down.

Even with the luxury of its reopening with decorative and compliant ladies, a fancy bar and dance floor, the wintry weather struck with enough destruction to disable the interior and discourage patrons. But while the Surf Point lasted, Gracie, Dick and Dan Poling, a former Marine and friend of Dick's who was a lawyer, would go to the Surf Point for fun and to lure customers to the Sea Hag. Dan sat in for the pianist often and Dick would climb up on the piano and sing Irish songs like Danny Boy and Mavoureen in such a touching voice that it moistened the eyes of the bar patrons. The performances came to a halt when one night Dick fell from the top of the piano and crashed on the keyboard, smashing Dan's fingers.

But during most nights, with the silent cooperation of Jake, the Surf Point bartender, Gracie would stand up and yell, "Yeah, come on with me. Free drinks at the Sea Hag!"

She'd empty the bar in no time and customers drove to the Sea Hag where, sure enough, they were served a free drink or two, then were on their own. Few stopped at one or two "tall ones." Many times a fun loving, serious drinking crowd would end up closing the Sea Hag at two thirty. Such maneuvers helped keep the Sea Hag afloat during the tough times and the lean years, for Gracie was always contriving new ways of attracting visitors to her restaurant.

People just loved her. She was a good sport when she fell victim to her customer's good-natured kidding. When Gracie had to lend a hand and serve drinks at the bar, a few of her "Steadies" called her the Wonder Bartender: "You wonder what you were going to get, wondered what it was going to cost and wondered who was going to get your change." She laughed along with her guests, and in return made them listen to her favorite joke of the moment. She loved to tell jokes. However she never got them right and totally wrecked them, including the punch line. But who would know? Cheeks dimpled, she plunged right in, and retold the joke in her own version, funnier than the original.

But in the silence of her private life, limited as it was, she had one single overriding concern. Her dark thoughts wove around Dick. Like his father before him, her husband had been diagnosed with Type 2 diabetes. This condition required a strict diet, no alcohol and exercise. Dick largely ignored the doctor's instructions and continued to drink heavily.

Gracie didn't pay much attention to Dick's consumption of alcohol. "I looked the other way," she said. "We were a generation who imbibed a lot, never got hangovers, and gave little thought to the consequences of a daily round of drinks. I'd been raised in a family where the men wore the pants, made the financial decisions and women went along where their husbands led. It was the way things were and while I knew Dick's dad had died as a result of diabetes, somehow I never put the two men in the same frame of reference. Except for tending bar at night, Dick didn't have much else to do with the running of the Sea Hag. The dining room was up to me, my kids and our few helpers."

❧∞❧

When things had a way of going too well, problems were born on the other side of "good," carried in on the wind and demanded Gracie's attention. A big problem made its way to the Sea Hag on sheets of heavy rain during one winter season. A big storm blew in to Depoe Bay the day before Thanksgiving 1965. A large holiday crowd was expected for the bountiful Thanksgiving buffet. But as Barbara, one of the old hands, put it, "God must have looked down on us and said to Himself, 'All this rain is a blessing so let's give them something to be thankful for.'"

One of the natural hazards of the heavy rains was the soaking of the hard-earth back lot, which years later was paved over and served as parking space for customers and employees. The big lot was located on an elevation rising about fifty feet above the Sea Hag building, so there was a natural incline for the rain to run down hill.

The first indication of trouble came one late afternoon after heavy rains swept in from the sea. A thick ooze of mud washed in and crept under the back door and down the hallway off the passage in the direction of the restrooms. Further along to the right was the door to the kitchen. The slimy mud draining the soaked soil from the flooded back lot seeped under the door and before the busy cook and dishwasher knew what was happening they were sliding around on the slippery floor trying in vain to stop the flood of dirty film with mops, brooms and rags. They succeeded only in smearing the floor and dispersing the mud under the stove, fridge, dishwasher, counter and food preparation tables.

To make matters worse, when Gracie was called, she took one look at the accumulating mess and called on help to block the runoff from sliding under the back door, the electricity went out. The Sea Hag was plunged into darkness. Used to emergencies, Gracie located the generator to restore light and blowers were brought in to dry the lingering moisture. This was after Gracie told her girls to connect a hose and flush the flowing muck out the front door and over the sidewalk curb where the rain would wash it into a storm drain.

It required one frantic day and blisters on hands to restore the Sea Hag to its normal spotless appearance with the work of Gracie, her kids, husband and three employees to wash, scrub and dry the floors. Primary attention was given to the dining area. Some of the meals were prepared on a camp stove installed in the kitchen while the stove area was being cleaned and ready to service. As far as Gracie recalled, no customers complained for they were unaware of the oozy flow in the kitchen where the mud had collected the thickest.

The emergency did not end with the mud removal effort. The crowd moving along the buffet tables was much larger than expected and Gracie could see the turkey wouldn't last. They'd need at least three fully roasted birds, ready to eat or they'd lose a lot of disappointed people. More than that, with the number of people coming through the front door for the buffet, the proceeds of the day, Gracie quickly calculated, would probably bring in enough income to carry the Sea Hag through the winter.

But where could she get large roasted turkeys? Her racing mind turned somersaults, when it dawned on Gracie that Coast Guard Chief Farmer was probably just about ready to sit down and carve his turkey, Gracie grabbed Barbara with instructions to bring a large platter with a cover, and ran out the door with her. Both women jumped in Gracie's car and whizzed down the street to the U.S. Coast Guard Station House. They walked into the spotless white, red-roofed building heading straight for the chief's room. Gracie knocked on the door and without waiting for a reply, charged in.

She was just in time, for Chief Farmer, ranking NCO in charge of the noncommissioned sailors based at Depoe Bay, was watching television where a big football game was going on, and on his table was a mouth-watering, roasted and stuffed twenty pound turkey. The Chief loved turkey and in the days after the holiday made sandwiches, turkey soup and picked the bird clean to the bone. He'd been waiting all day for his dinner. Turkey was his favorite food and he had prepared it lovingly, cooking it slowly, basting it carefully in anticipation of how good it was going to taste.

"When we burst through his door and cried, "Chief, could we have your turkey? We've got a full house of customers and we're out of turkey."

He blinked, surprise washed over his features, and he muttered, "My turkey?"

"Yes, please, and come to the Sea Hag and have your dinner on the house there. We'll buy you another turkey and cook it for you besides."

"He sighed, looked at his bird lovingly, and nodded his head.

The duo located two other roasted turkeys at the home of the Wickes, a family who we interrupted before they could slice their turkey. They, too, surrendered their holiday bird, two in this case, responding to the urgency in Gracie's voice and the power of her irresistible presence.

Gracie never forgot the generosity of those people. They recognized the dilemma the Sea Hag faced and how their gift would save the day in the spirit of Thanksgiving.

Gracie and her dog,
Jack, 1938

Gracie's Parents, 1926

Gracie, 1942

Gracie in shades, 1946

*Gracie and Pauline,
1944*

Depoe Bay, Postcard, 1936

Cute teen, 1946

Gracie: Going my way? 1946

Depoe Bay, Postcard, 1936

Ski Bunny, 1947

Singing in the rain,1946

Gracie's family, 1948

Gracie and Dick, 1948

*Gracie at Fairchild
Field, 1949*

*Gracie and Dick,
Wedding couple,
1949*

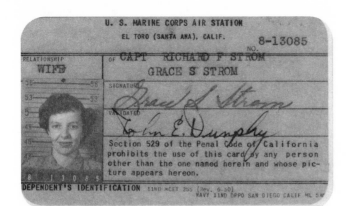

*Gracie's
I.D. Card,
1952*

*Dick and the kids
with his airplane,
1956*

*The Sea Hag,
tavern,
1950s*

The kids at Christmas, 1958

The Poop Deck Room, 1960s

The Sea Hag, 1960s

The family,
1959

First Sea Hag
meal, 1963

Helicopter
wreckage,
1960

Chapter 4

It was on a dry day during the same winter season that Gracie, aware of leaks in the flat roof when heavy rain ate its way through the roofing material, dripping through the ceiling, confronted the mean-spirited man who operated a candy shop in the same building next door to the Sea Hag. He was responsible for sabotaging the newly coated flat roof for which Gracie had just hired a man to apply a layer of hot tar to seal the surface against water penetration.

When, after the roof had been waterproofed, a new storm thundered in from the sea dumping rain in windy gushes on the roof, Gracie was beside herself. A flood of water had poured down from the rear end of the roof, churned through the back door of the Sea Hag and down the hallway to the kitchen. Water surged in a wave three inches deep that flooded the kitchen and restaurant. She called in a plumber who told her she needed to get her roof fixed and he "Red-Tagged" the Sea Hag for delinquent maintenance.

The Red Tag was in effect an order to shut down the Sea Hag until the leaks had been fixed. Also, Gracie learned from the plumber that the owner of English Taffy Shop next door had complained of water damage in his shop coming from the Sea Hag. As soon as the weather cleared and the restaurant was dry again from the efforts of the family and loyal employees, Gracie, suspicious that the drainpipes from the roof might have deliberately been plugged, examined them carefully. On the roof she discovered that the drain openings had been sealed shut with hot tar. When it cooled and became solid it was rock hard and closed the water exits from the roof. She knew without a doubt who had done it.

Furious, fearless and determined, Gracie stormed out of the front door of the Sea Hag. She flung open the neighboring door to the English Taffy Shop and confronted the mean-eyed, middle-aged owner whose face wore a permanent sour expression of craftiness, discontent and spitefulness. His mouth was tight from lack of smiling and looked as though the man had swallowed his lips. His name was Ainslee. Before she opened her mouth to accuse him of deliberately clogging the drains, she saw the guilt and triumph in his eyes. His face changed when she charged in a low voice, "You mean bastard, I know what you did on the roof and I'm going to tell the plumbing inspector whom I've called exactly what kind of miserable soul you are. If you ever do something like that again, I don't think I could keep my friends from coming over and teaching you a lesson." As she turned to leave, she saw fear on the hateful features of the conniving old man.

When the inspector called on Gracie and she relayed to him that Ainslee was responsible for the damage on the roof, he shook his head regretfully. "I'm so sorry you've got such a neighbor. I'm taking down that Red Tag," he said. "Anybody who would be that mean, who would pull that kind of shenanigans on you, well, to hell with him."

Gracie could never answer the question of why such hate motivated a person to deliberately cause trouble for another human being. She settled on the simple explanation that he was just a mean soul, probably eaten up with disappointments and turned his failures into malice for others.

Gracie knew the girl the Ainslees had adopted, because they could not have children of their own, hated them. Mrs. Ainslee would never allow anybody to come into their home because they might dirty it. She was the kind who had the family laundry all labeled. Like her husband, she was just plain mean. Their adopted daughter ran away when she was only twelve. She had reached the point where she could not stand to be near them. Not long after the incident, Gracie heard that when the bitter old man had died, his widow found a decent man and − miracle upon miracle − changed into a loving woman.

There was always some kind of drama being played out at the Sea Hag that few customers ever heard of. Those who worked closely with Gracie and her girls were more involved and part of the family atmosphere of the Sea Hag. Loyal and true, they were always on hand to save the day.

❧

Dishwashers at the Sea Hag were called "ceramic engineers," even though the exaggerated title did not add much prestige to the job. Dishwashers came and went and for a transient guy or girl hard up for a job, it put money into empty pockets and regular meals in their growling stomachs.

All kinds of characters wandered off Highway 101 and just like a magnet attracting metal, headed straight into the lap of the Sea Hag. True to the old saying that people are God's zoo, the variety of human critters that passed through the doors of Gracie's place were as colorful and unique as the workings of a kaleidoscope. Like in a theatre, comedy and tragedy played out under life's direction at the Sea hag

There was Luther, who worked as a dishwasher at the restaurant and always brought his Bible with him. He took it into the kitchen and read from it when ever he had a break. Luther underlined quotations and preached to the staff whenever somebody would listen. He read from his Bible and talked about how close he was to his mother and how fond he was of her. With a sad tone of voice he informed the Sea Hag crew one night that she had died − she had just suddenly and unexpectedly passed away.

He seemed heartbroken when he told his girlfriend about his mother's death. He had promised to marry her after his mother was gone. For some strange reason, he confessed to her that he had smothered his mother. In other words, he had murdered her.

Nobody thought that there was anything strange about his mother's death because she'd been sickly and bed ridden for quite some time. She was sleeping when he placed a pillow over her face one night. However, he made a big mistake of telling his girlfriend to go fly a kite. He told her in no uncertain terms, that he wasn't about to spend his mother's good money on her and reneged on a promised trip to Disneyland. Furious as any woman scorned, angry because he had failed to keep his word, the former love of his life contacted the authorities and they fixed her up with a wire so she could record whatever Luther would tell her.

That very day she confronted him, "I know you killed your mother," she started out, "and you promised to give me some money. I want my share."

"It's just your word against mine," Luther replied with a sneer. "She's long dead and buried now. It's been almost a year. There's no way you could prove I killed her. She just died in her sleep."

"You know good and well, you told me you smothered her, with a pillow."

"So what if I did," he retorted hotly, "You're still not getting a dime of the money, that's it."

That was enough.

The police arrested him and, faced with the recording of admitting killing his mother, Luther pleaded guilty and was sentenced to a long prison term.

"We thought he was a simple, ordinary guy and such a good Christian," Gracie pondered. "Here was a fellow who washed dishes at our kitchen for years, lectured to us from his Bible and did his best to convert us. We just never suspected he was a killer."

And the human drama kept on playing out at Gracie's place. She described another employee, a girl who worked tending bar and ended up being murdered. Her mother worked for the Sea Hag also as a waitress, and her daughter was an adorable girl, friendly and quite popular. Everyone at the restaurant liked her. One night, after the girl got off work, she went down to the Pip Tide, an old bar in Newport on the waterfront, known for its gambling tables, loud music and as a hangout for hippies.

When the young woman didn't come home, Gracie took over and called all over town trying to find her. Over and over she was told that the girl had left the Pip Tide and had gone down to the jetty in the company of a couple of men whom everyone knew — brothers they said.

"We knew these brothers," Gracie reminisced, "and several of us went to see those fellows who lived in a trailer with their mother at the end of town. We knocked on their door and asked them if they knew where our girl was, since we'd heard she'd left the Pip Tide with them. The men were rude, told us to get off their premises and not show our faces again. However, they admitted they had had a big row with her."

At a loss of where to look anymore, the missing girl's mother called the police and the search began immediately. The police issued an all-points bulletin, and early the next day, her crumpled, lifeless body was found sprawled on the rocks of the jetty. She'd been raped and murdered. Strangled.

"We had to be the bearers of the terrible news to her mother who was supposed to be at work that day as was her daughter," Gracie recalled with sadness in her voice. "Come to find out, the two brothers had taken her from the Pip Tide, raped her and killed her right there on the jetty. The girl's killers must have assumed the darkness would hide their shameful deed and the breaking waves would wash the corpse out into the sea. But it hadn't worked out that way. The dead girl resisted the ocean's pull — clung to the rocks to bear witness to the foul play."

Gracie remembered another violent death involving a roving bartender, the husband of one of the Sea Hag's waitresses. His name was Tank — a big Teddy-Bear-type of guy. Tank worked in a tavern, called the Sloop John B. on the new mall in Depoe Bay, which Gracie and her friends had developed. He was without a doubt an excellent bartender, and ran a terrific bar. Everybody loved him. He didn't come home the night he won a contest for the Ugliest Bartender in Oregon from the Restaurant Association of Portland. He just disappeared. Nobody could find him. It had been one of those cold foggy nights on the coast where everything was hidden behind a thick, white wall. It was easy to get lost.

Two days after he disappeared, the Coast Guard found his car submerged at North Point. Just the top of the automobile was visible with waves washing over it. He had drowned because he was unable to get out of the vehicle after running over a clif in the fog. There was no way for anybody to get down to the car even at low tide. To remove it from the ocean, a big derrick was brought in which hoisted the auto up from the bottom of the cliff. When they found Tank behind the wheel, everyone agreed sadly that he must have celebrated winning the Ugliest Bartender Contest with a whole lot of drinks. He was alone in the car when coming home and took a wrong turn in the fog.

Tank's wife was inconsolable and desperate for they had no money saved. But as an employer, Gracie carried a $10,000 insurance policy that covered those who died while on the Sea Hag payroll. Payment of the policy was withheld for a while until the insurance company was satisfied to rule out suicide. Tank's widow was given a total of $20,000 for his accidental death. Had Tank had been wearing a seat belt the amount would have been $30,000. Never accused of being shy, after handing the check over to the widow, Gracie informed the insurance company they were cheapskates for trying to dodge payment. The policy stipulated that an employee had to die while he was working on the job to be eligible for compensation.

The years of the Sea Hag, like the dependable ocean, just a stone's throw away, rolled together in a seamless stream of days that were all the same, but different. Sometime in the early 70s, Gracie and two logger friends bought an establishment, called the Tuckaway Inn. The place was located in Hebo some forty miles inland from Depoe Bay on the Nestucka River – a village hardly big enough to spit across. A Country and Western band supplied the entertainment attracting the loggers from around who were steady customers. The band was composed of loggers from Portland and their exuberant, hand-clapping, foot-stomping performances packed in the crowds who liked the rural atmosphere. People loved that old Hebo inn, with its beer bottle-shaped fridge that contained a plentiful supply of favorite brews. The old inn was a three-story building where the rooms on the second and third floors sported one light bulb in the middle of the ceiling, an ancient sink and one bathroom at the end of the hall on the second and third floor. The salmon and steelhead in the river called to well-to-do fishermen who would come to catch the wild fish. They'd stay in those old rooms for about five dollars a night.

When Gracie bought the place she wanted to change its name to a more clever, catchy one. Since the building contained all those rooms upstairs, she kept with the Tuckaway Inn. She needed this catchy marketing tool because after she bought the place she discovered that the floors were pitched at such a slant that if a guest stepped out in the hallway and it was wet outside, he'd slide right out onto the deck and literally land on his face.

For those days, Gracie thought the slant was clever, and was certainly aware the rooms hosted many couples who replaced the letter "T" of the Tuckaway Inn with the letter "F." She had never used that word in her life, but the men who brought their women would fling it about freely; the name became kind of a joke and it stuck.

As the new owner taking care of her business, Gracie would make the trip from Depoe Bay to Hebo after working the day at the Sea Hag, tending bar at the inn at night. It was strictly a sort of farm-like tavern but it had the only liquor license in town and harbored a great history in its frail, old walls. Portlanders flocked to that lonely, quaint spot in the road to do their steelhead fishing because they got consistent results and the lack of formality at the inn was comfortable. The Tuckaway offered a blend of rustic, primitive and homey.

Running two restaurants was demanding enough, but driving each day almost one hundred miles on the narrow two-lane country roads between the two establishments had become a nuisance, and was beginning to be a strain on Gracie. But once again, it was the new innkeeper's personality that kept the crowds coming. Then opportunity knocked on her door. A wealthy lady, who visited the inn often with her boyfriend and spent the night, offered to buy the place for the man in her life who always wanted to own a bar. The woman never haggled about the price, paid the full fare and a load dropped off of Gracie's shoulders. She admitted that she never would have had the courage to buy the inn in the first place had it not been for two men who came into her life who were wise about real estate. And, as the years would witness, in the company of John Holliday and Jim Cutler her real estate holdings not only were sound investments but also changed the face of Depoe Bay.

The budding entrepreneur never gave failure a thought, jumped right in when the wind was right and the tide rolled in on time. It should not have come as a surprise when son, Larry, turned out to be an entrepreneur in his own right. By the time he was thirteen, he had turned into a sharp and enterprising kid and started in the business of pickling fish. His mentor was John Holiday, a logger who was his mother's friend and mentor. He taught Larry a lot. Larry pickled salmon in big jars and sold it at a market they set up in Depoe Bay.

"He was just a high school kid," Gracie laughed and continued, "I was at the market one day when one of the little old ladies who was a customer pointed to a fresh salmon filet and said, 'I want that filet over there.'

Larry, never correcting her, asked, 'Which one?'

"'Oh, this one.'

"He wrapped that filet, never once referring to her mistake.

Larry's fish market turned out to be quite successful and by the time he was sixteen he had a thriving business supplying not only the Sea Hag's growing needs but other restaurants and the public.

She also remembers the model airplane shop Larry had as a pre-teen, making and selling model airplanes. This early love of airplanes would grow throughout his life. Gracie's eyes turned wistful when she remembered those long ago days. "I was proud of him for his business sense and a lot of other things. The little old ladies just loved him. Everybody stopped to buy pickled fish from Larry. We built a nice building there and added smoked fish to sell."

Larry was the son, Gracie said, who would return because when he left college, he went to welding school in Portland. "He said to me one day, 'Every time I come back to Depoe Bay, people always stop me and say You're Gracie's son? You never mentioned you had a son.' They always knew the girls, my sisters, but, 'Gracie never mentioned you.' Thanks Mom for not telling anybody about me."

Because Larry was so industrious and busy with his own enterprises, people didn't see him as much as the girls, both of whom worked at the Sea Hag. But he was inventive and helped engineer the building of the smokehouse for the fish market. Larry smoked salmon, tuna and halibut – fish prepared in a different way, including the soon to be popular teriyaki-smoked salmon. "He ran the operation all by himself, and I know," Gracie smiled, "he was proud. He'd come home with the day's take in a white sandwich sack.

Then came the weekend when he did not hand his money to his mother. It turned out that he had placed the bag with the money on top of the dishwasher in the kitchen at the Sea Hag. The bag was gone.

"We looked all through everything," Gracie recalled. "Finally we decided, the sack had been thrown in the garbage. We didn't know for sure. There were always a lot of kids around and someone may have taken it. But we decided that the money had landed in the garbage and took off for the garbage dump. I told the man in charge of the county dump that we'd lost something we needed badly and we started digging through all that muck. Pretty soon, we looked like the people who owned that dump; they always had black faces.

"It was an amazing expedition. We found lots of money, cartons of cigarettes probably discarded when their owners stopped smoking. We came across some beautiful dolls and some of the oddest things that gave me a whole new insight into people's lives. And, there were rats scurrying all over the mountains of garbage. Oh, it was horrible! We never did find the money sack. After we left the dump of digging all through the garbage, the word got out that what we'd lost was highly valuable. As a result a whole crowd of people headed for the dump we had left empty-handed and started digging. If someone had found the money bag he would have been seven hundred dollars richer."

The police moved in on the case of the missing money because Gracie had reported the loss to the authorities. As a result everyone at the Sea Hag had to take a lie detector test. Ridiculous as it may seem, only daughter Sally and Gracie's best friend, Jim Cutler, flunked the test. "We were all under suspicion," Sally remembered, "because everything we did at work ended up in a white paper bag, including the money."

There was the night, when Gerry, the bartender, before closing, ordered food and placed what she couldn't eat into a white take-out bag. When she finished her shift and closed the bar, she made a mistake. She had put her leftover dinner into the safe in the floor. Later, she grabbed the nearest white paper bag from the safe, and instead of taking her leftover dinner home she had a bag full of money when she reached home. She was not the only one who handled money in a most casual way. Jim Cutler would often take the night's receipts home with him, after he had been drinking, and more than once a white paper bag with money would be found in the parking lot where he had dropped it getting into his car

As for Gracie, when she left the dump after her search party came up empty-handed, she confessed that she'd had the best time. She could not believe how much good stuff people discarded. She came home with all sorts of junky treasures. On the other hand, Gracie – like a kid at Christmas – almost always had a good time. Her children will vouch for that.

❧

Young Larry took after his industrious parents and contributed to the family earnings by going into his own business, He attended high school until noon. Then each day, he headed for the waterfront to buy crabs and fish from the big companies. He'd sell some of the crab live and brought the rest of the squiggly lot home, which he placed into the big crab pots and cooked them. The Chinese and Japanese population loved fresh crab – they were especially fond of the inner part, which they called the "butter in the crab." They bought crab by the dozen from Larry right out of the cooker.

Larry's big smokers processed salmon – the undisputed king of the fish. One way to get salmon really cheap was to go out at midnight in a rowboat and throw gillnets out across the Siletz River not far from the Sea Hag when the law wasn't around. Well, Gracie admitted if she ever stole anything like salmon, she'd be a nervous wreck knowing she'd get caught and thrown in jail. She went out with her gillnetting friends only one time. She was given the job of rowing their little old rowboat, when all of a sudden her friends kept warning her, "Watch out for a game guy about."

"They're never around at midnight," she had been told, "but you never can tell." It was like that old game we used to do as kids – we played False Alarm. But Gracie had all she wanted of illegal adventures – harmless as they may have been – and started rowing that boat toward shore as fast as she could paddle and broke the oar in two. Her gillnetting attempts were over. To this day she is a nervous wreck, just thinking about the possibility of getting caught.

The year was 1967 and even though the Sea Hag was still on shaky ground, the place was making its way and was growing more and more popular after four years under Dick and Gracie's care.

Home life was as hectic as the Strom's time at work. Just like the ocean rolling to shore in lines of waves, retreating and forming new walls of white-crested green glass, so did one day run into the other bringing new challenges including tending to the demands of three growing children. Dick and Gracie spent little time together. That's why Dick's sentimental surprise he sprang on Gracie meant so much more. They two had been married in a civil ceremony on July 27, 1949 and their eighteenth anniversary was around the corner.

Gracie had not questioned Dick's absence once a month for a couple of hours, but discovered his secret a few days before their anniversary. Gracie was just about out the door on her way to work when Dick stopped her and quietly announced, "We're getting married on our anniversary in the Catholic Church."

Gracie was speechless and deeply touched when he confessed that he had been meeting once a month with Father Radakowski, a local priest who loved his wine. At their meeting, the two men headed for the Townhouse, a quiet place that served wine and discussed the philosophy of the Catholic Church. The owners of the Townhouse always treated Father Radakowski to food and over a glass or two of golden liquid, the priest instructed Dick how he could achieve a state of grace that would allow the Catholic Church to bind marriage vows between him and Gracie.

"Father Radakowski is going to marry us at Sacred Heart Church in Newport. I'm not sure if you can receive Holy Communion, but you can still be a Catholic," Dick announced, pleased as Punch that his surprise had overwhelmed his bride of eighteen years.

Moved to happy tears, Gracie couldn't believe her husband had arranged a church-blessed marriage after all those years. With excited members of the family and friends including their next door neighbors, Bud and Mary Kuhlenbeck, looking on, the couple was married in the age-old tradition of the Catholic Church — flowers, blessings, tears, champagne and all.

And as prescribed by tradition, after the ceremony, the once-again newlyweds left on their honeymoon, and the Strom children proudly announced at school that their mother and father had just gotten married. The news was a bit of a puzzle to the parents of some of the kids with whom Nancy, Larry and Sally were friends. Living together without benefit of a ceremony was frowned on a bit even in the sixties. The three children hadn't mentioned the previous union by a justice of the peace. But none of that mattered to Gracie, she was her own person and rarely looked for acceptance or approval for her life style. Her world was a blend of many colors melding into each other in blissful harmony. And it was the power of that harmony that made a difference in the lives of people — especially the ones who worked for her.

The restaurant business is notorious for waiters, cooks and all to be short-term employees. Like birds on the wing, they go from place to place looking for what, they don't know, but not so at Depoe Bay's Sea Hag.

Of all of the people who worked at the Sea Hag, one who stayed until she no longer could work and was more like a member of the family than an employee, was of course, Nellie Munson, the cook. Gracie readily acknowledged that Nellie literally raised the Strom kids. Everybody loved her. There was a bit of sadness about her, because she had no children She desperately wanted somebody of her very own to love. And every time a stray dog was injured on the highway, out she'd go to save the animal or bury it in a graveyard in the lot back of the Sea Hag. There were so many dogs buried there that the grass was always green. Every time one of the kid's dogs was killed on the highway it was heartbreak time at the Sea Hag.

Like most children, the Strom kids wanted to have a dog around. "Did we let them have a dog?" Gracie chuckled. "Yes, we did. We had probably more than twenty dogs. There were St. Bernards, police dogs, wolf dogs – big ones and small ones, furry ones and slick ones. We had every dog in the book and some who weren't. And," she continued slowly, "we never had a dog that died of old age, except for Ivan." He, too, had been a victim of highway traffic.

Sally had rescued the injured animal and rushed him to the vet who announced the dog had a broken hip and needed surgery only performed by some specialist in the state of Washington. So much for that! The cost of the operation and the money needed to travel were exorbitant and out of the question. The next best thing to do was to take him to Nellie who liked nothing better than to nurse a broken critter back to life. Ivan recovered and it took him no time to adjust to getting around on three legs. Unfortunately, the dog quickly became the dogcatcher's favorite target, causing Gracie to go to court to plead his case in front of a judge. Except for the fact she had to pay a ten-dollar fine more than once for the dog's lack of respect for the law, Ivan was no trouble and turned out to be the ideal family pet. She told the judge that the dogcatcher had a personal vendetta with Ivan and went out of his way to catch him.

Gracie must have presented Ivan's case with such overwhelming passion and well timed irresistible humor – making the dogcatcher the villain of the drama – that Judge Huckleberry suggested she approach City Council asking them to get rid of the menace. Gracie triumphed: The dogcatcher was fired and the beloved pets of Depoe Bay were once again able to roam the streets and beaches, or as Gracie, their benefactress, put it "free to stroll and visit their friends, not to mention showing up regularly at the Sea Hag during Sunday brunch."

There was always something happening at the Sea Hag. The bar was open until 2:30 in the morning and on slow nights Gracie played pinochle with the loggers at a table by the fireplace in the bar, where the dancing flames of the cheery fire threw flickering shadows on the walls. Since the loggers insisted on playing for money Gracie quickly learned not to overbid her hand since it could mean losing a twenty-dollar bill. Those loggers didn't play for fun.

One late night, absorbed in the game, the pinochle players didn't look up from their cards until somebody yelled that a small river of bubbly, soapy water was rushing down the hall and was pouring into the bar. Somebody in the kitchen had filled the sink in preparation for washing dishes, left and had forgotten to turn off the water. The card game came to an abrupt halt. Someone splashed through the ankle-deep water to shut off the forgotten faucet and the rest of the group ran for mops and buckets to cleanup the mess.

The Sea Hag was the kind of place that attracted and played to all kinds of audiences. There was the night when a tourist caused a great deal of trouble, something he would painfully regret. Apparently the man not only liked his booze but he enjoyed playing nasty jokes on people. He was sitting at one of the small tables near the door and every time some one walked by, he stuck out his foot to trip the unsuspecting individual and sent him flying face down to the floor. He'd laugh his head off as he watched the surprised look on his victim's face, struggling to get back on his feet. He did his despicable little trick several times until he met up with destiny when Nellie's husband, Butch, came through the door.

Butch, was a fisherman, a little short guy, but ornery as could be. He walked by the man's table, stumbled over his foot, but luckily, he caught himself before falling. Butch took one look at the smirk on the man's face and knocked him through the wall with his fist. When the joker came out of his daze, he stood up unsteadily, shook his head to clear the cobwebs, mumbled something unintelligible and made a dash for the door.

Then there was always the guy who'd arrive all tanked up already, was refused another drink and in his hazy stage would express his disappointment in different ways. Some would whine and plead and flatter the bartender in order to wheedle another shot or two out of her. Some were verbally abusive, used foul language, yelled and hollered until they were escorted out the door by the scruff of the neck. The next category belongs to the bullies – the ugly drunks. When Barbara Mason was tending bar one night a tall man came into the bar, drunk, with a fixed intensity in his face and a wildness in his eyes. One look at the man was enough for Barbara to say in a gentle tone, "I'm sorry sir, I can't serve you."

He just looked at her, and without uttering a word picked up the ashtrays off the bar and threw them into the row of bottles lined up against the mirrored wall of the bar. Barbara freaked out and yelled, "Somebody call 911!" Before anybody could get there, the wild man tossed a drink down her back.

Since there were no cops around for miles, it took them a while to get there. Fortunately, a Coastie came to the rescue, held on to the man and calmed him down until the police finally arrived. It turned out that the troublemaker had escaped from an asylum in Salem. He just went wild.

"The hardest thing in the world to do in a bar is to shut somebody off. Telling the customer he can't have another drink, that is tough," Barbara Lanagan chipped in.

Then there was the problem of fixing fancy drinks, some of which had more ingredients than a shark has teeth. Gracie got to be an expert at changing patrons' minds about the mixed drinks they ordered if they were too difficult for her to make. Royal Gin Fizzes and fancy concoctions were discouraged. When she couldn't avoid making a Royal Gin Fizz, she'd line up the egg, the gin, orange juice and the sour mix. With a lot of hand and arm activity, she'd take the whole egg and throw it in the mix without cracking it and turn the blender on – eggshell and all.   "Hey, weren't you supposed to separate that egg?" questioned the astonished customer.

"No," Gracie replied, as smooth as the creamy fizz and with authority, "this gives you calcium with your drink." When the egg goes through the blender, Gracie elaborated that it didn't hurt anybody. It never did. No one can taste the shells. If nothing else, it sure discouraged a few people from believing that's not really the way to do it.

"Another polite turn off for making a complicated fancy drink was the excuse that the blender was broken. Then of course I always pulled the deal about salting the rim of the glass to make a Margarita blended instead of on the rocks. It was so much work to blend it that I'd always lick the rim of the glass with my tongue and then salt it. The alert barfly changed his mind quickly and would say, "Oh forget about it, I'll take it on the rocks." Naughty Gracie would get a surprised look on her face, grin slyly, and happily fix that Margarita on the rocks.

Her staff never forgot the day Gracie sat down with a couple who came to the restaurant, talked up a storm, soon called them by their first names and offered them a piece of (day-old) chocolate pie. Norm and Phyllis Johnson politely refused. The hostess kept insisting and again the couple declined. No one knew what came over Gracie, but in between talking she vigorously attacked the chocolate pie and polished the whole thing off. Not a crumb was left. No explanation, except: "Well, that's Gracie!" The latter handled the whole affair with her usual wide-eyed, innocent grin, enhanced by her so-what's-wrong-with-that attitude?

It was near the five-year mark since the Stroms had bought the Sea Hag when Gracie began to be concerned with Dick's fits of moodiness and his heavy drinking at home. He sat for long periods in his favorite chair, often staring into space always with a drink in his hand. During his bartending shifts at the Sea Hag he'd often talk to a former Marine officer, now a local attorney, who like himself served in World War II. Their common background strengthened the bond of friendship. Also Dick's oldest daughter, Nancy, sensitive to her father's increasing periods of depression, would on many occasions sit with him for hours at the house and listened when he reminisced about his flying days in World War II and his bombing runs into North Korea during that subsequent conflict.

It was his activities in Korea that troubled him with a deep sense of guilt for the blameless North Korean civilians his bombing raids killed. In one of his talks with Nancy, he told her about an outstanding pilot, Butch O'Hare, who earlier had been based on the same aircraft carrier, the *Lexington*, from which Dick had also flown missions.

Dick had given Nancy two typewritten pages. One described the achievements of Butch O'Hare and the other was a different, but related story. Several years later, Nancy sent Gracie copies of the stories for the family file she was making.

One day O'Hare's entire squadron was sent on a mission. After he was airborne, he looked at his fuel gauge and realized that someone had forgotten to top off his tank. He would not have enough fuel to complete his mission and get back to his ship. His flight leader told him to return to the carrier. Reluctantly, he dropped out of formation and headed back to the fleet. As he was returning to the mother ship he saw something that turned his blood cold, a squadron of Japanese aircraft was speeding its way toward the American fleet. The American fighters were gone on a sortie, and the fleet was all but defenseless. He couldn't reach his squadron and bring them back in time to save the fleet. Nor could he warn the fleet of the approaching danger. There was only one thing to do. He must somehow divert them from the fleet.

Laying aside all thoughts of personal safety, he dove into the formation of Japanese planes. Wing-mounted 50-calibers blazed as he charged in, attacking one surprised enemy plane and then another. Butch wove in and out of the now broken formation and fired at as many planes as possible until all his ammunition was finally spent. Undaunted, he continued the assault. He dove at the planes, trying to clip a wing or tail in hopes of damaging as many enemy planes as possible and rendering them unfit to fly. Finally, the demoralized Japanese squadron took off in another direction.

Deeply relieved, Butch O'Hare and his bullet-riddled fighter limped back to the carrier. Upon arrival he reported in and related the event surrounding his return. The film from the gun-camera mounted on his plane told the tale. It showed Butch's daring attempt to protect his fleet. He had in fact destroyed five enemy aircraft. This took place on February 20, 1942, and for that action Butch became the Navy's first Ace of World War II, and the first Naval Aviator to win the Congressional Medal of Honor. A year later, Butch was killed in aerial combat at the age of 29. His hometown would not allow the memory of this World War II hero to fade, and today, O'Hare Airport in Chicago is named in tribute to the courage of this great man. A sculpture of Butch O'Hare can be seen at the airport named after him.

"That's a good story," Nancy had said to her father, "but you were a hero too, with a Silver Star and a Gold Medal in lieu of a second one. Tell me the other story that's related to Butch O'Hare."

Only too happy to have an audience for his stories, Dick wasted no time and spun his next tale.

"It happened even before Butch was born, but you'll understand after I tell how it fits."

Many years ago, probably before O'Hare Field was built, Al Capone virtually owned Chicago. Capone wasn't famous for anything heroic. He was notorious for enmeshing the windy city in everything from bootlegged booze and prostitution to murder. Capone had a lawyer nicknamed "Easy Eddie." He was his lawyer for a good reason. Eddie was very good! In fact, Eddie's skill at legal maneuvering kept Big Al out of jail for a long time. To show his appreciation, Capone paid him very well. Not only was the money big, but also Eddie got special dividends. For instance, he and his family occupied a fenced-in mansion with live-in help and all of the conveniences of the day. The estate was so large that it filled an entire Chicago city block. Eddie lived the high life of the Chicago mob and gave little consideration to the crime that went on around him.

'Eddie did have one soft spot, however. He had a son that he loved dearly. Eddie saw to it that his young son had the best of everything: clothes, cars and a good education. Nothing was withheld. Price was no object. And, despite his involvement with organized crime, Eddie even tried to teach him right from wrong. Eddie wanted his son to be a better man than he was. Yet, with all his wealth and influence, there were two things he couldn't give his son; he couldn't pass on a good name and a good example.

"One day, Easy Eddie reached a difficult decision. He wanted to rectify wrongs he had done. He decided he would go to the authorities and tell the truth about Al "Scarface" Capone, clean up his tarnished name and offer his son some semblance of integrity. To do this, he would have to testify against The Mob, and he knew that the cost would be great. So, he testified. Within the year, Easy Eddie's life ended in a blaze of gunfire on a lonely Chicago street. But in his eyes, he had given his son the greatest gift he had to offer, and the greatest price he would ever pay. Police removed from his pockets a rosary, a crucifix, a religious medallion and a poem clipped from a magazine. The poem read: *The clock of life is wound but once. And no man has the power To tell just when the hands will stop At late or early hour. Now is the only time you own.*

"I bet you can guess the name of Eddie's son? 'Dick stopped for a second. "Yep, it was Butch O'Hare."

Just as Dick's storytelling kept his children spellbound at home, his audiences at the Sea Hag bar used to hang on his every word, drinks clutched in their hands and kept those short and tall ones coming for Dick. The large amounts of alcohol he consumed may have added sparkle to his lively storytelling, but in reality it became a depressant and only contributed to his sense of loss and exaggerated despair of the part he played in Korea.

Chapter 5

Just as storm-laden clouds gather at the horizon and move steadily towards the shore to spend themselves in torrential downpours and whip-like gusts of wind, so did foul-weather signs hang low and threatening over the Sea Hag. They held the promise of rough times ahead. It was not an empty promise.

It was in 1968 that Dick's heavy, daily drinking did not go unnoticed. The Sea Hag's liquor license was in serious jeopardy and inevitably was behind his decision to check into an alcohol rehabilitation center in Portland. The "drying out" treatment was an act of desperation for him, for though he endured the twenty-eight-day sobering up cycle, never once was he convinced that he could break the habit. His state of depression had become so chronic that his only relief was the knowledge he was contributing to the major income source of the Sea Hag.

But one evening when he closed the bar, he kept shaking his head, "Grace," he said, "I've tried, but I can't lick this alcohol thing. And today my doctor told me, 'Dick you're already showing the symptoms of diabetic complications, if you don't stop drinking, I can't give you more than six months before you'll be unable to walk. In a year or sooner, you'll lose both of your legs to neuropathy. You're father died from diabetic complications. Unless you want to end your life the same way, you'll have to follow a strict regimen of no booze, a prescribed diet and increasing daily exercise. Dick, this is my last warning. You may not be around for another.'"

Silence. The only sound was the roll and tumble of the incoming tide as the waves washed over the sand under a dark night sky.

The pain that threatened to crush Gracie's heart and soul was a deeper shock than Dick could imagine, when he told her he was giving up on life. He couldn't lick his alcohol addiction. She knew he already experienced pain and numbness in his legs, but she was convinced he could cure himself if he followed the doctor's instructions. Or could he? He had just confessed to her that he couldn't kick the booze.

With an old sadness clouding her eyes, Gracie began to talk about the past. "Suddenly, I was faced with a grim future in which my husband wouldn't be around. I didn't know what to say. I felt a deep chill and a desperate sorrow rushing up within me. I knew that his drinking was creating a serious problem for our business because the Liquor Commission would not renew our license. It was issued in both our names originally and it was the lifeblood of our business. It was suggested to put the liquor license in my name only because they were afraid that if anything happened – an accident with Dick driving drunk, or anything that could be blamed on excessive alcohol consumption, our license would be pulled. We couldn't have that on our record, because alcohol distribution is a pretty strict state-controlled operation. They were adamant about it. And the owners of the Sea Hag's building were also quite nervous. They had health problems of their own and had the building for sale for a long time. The asking price to Gracie and Dick was $60,000. That was a lot of money at that time.

"And as far as the license went, Oregon was not like California where you simply bought a liquor license. Here it's more like goodwill, yet restrictive to whom they would give the privilege of selling alcohol. Tavern licenses to sell beer and wine were easily available, but liquor licenses were hard to come by and were handed out on a quota system.

"Our license came with the Sea Hag. We didn't buy the building; we just bought the business. We had been looking for a business opportunity, something with which we were familiar. My theory was based on the fact that that we'd logged many hours on the patron side of a bar, but not behind it, it was something we would do. We'd had many years experience drinking and we both thought it would be enjoyable. The Sea Hag fit our plans of running a restaurant and bar in a tourist area. The only problem, at that time in Oregon, was that visitors rarely came to the coast except in summer – four or five months at the most. The rest of the year we prayed and hoped that the locals and traveling salesmen would keep us going. The summer business was just fantastic. We looked at a lot of places, but we liked the Sea Hag best. There was something about that place that made it attractive to us. And it worked."

Gracie stopped for a moment and when she continued, her voice was hesitant and low, her face showed sharp edges of sadness and unshed tears hovered in her eyes.

Without a warning to Gracie, her husband decided to end his life on February 14, 1968.

According to Nancy, her mother never talked about his suicide. "Sometimes when we revisited the tragic event as a family, we always thought 'Was I there when that happened?' We all have our own version of how it happened. I knew he was an alcoholic. Dad locked the bedroom door when he wanted to be alone and Mom used to try to get into their room with a hanger because the door had a chain-lock. I remember hearing Mom messing around with the lock until it unlocked and she could open the door. I was in the bathroom adjacent to the bedroom, when I heard her scream.

She had found Dick slumped over on the side of the bed; he had shot himself in the head. She came running into the hall with a gun in her hand and some blood spatters on her. She was hyster-ical, screaming and I had no idea what was going on. I rushed into

Dad's room and, horrified, I saw him lying there — dead. Larry and Sally appeared in the hall; the noise had woken them up. My brother went into the bedroom while I tried to keep Sally out of there; I didn't want her to see what had happened.

"I remember Mother, dressed in a little negligee, waving the bloody gun wildly in the air and saying, 'I'm going to kill myself. I can't live with this. I can't do this!' Mom was running out the front door holding onto the gun, still shouting she was going to kill herself. It was a crazy scene. I had just gotten out of the shower, so I wasn't dressed either. I had hurriedly wrapped myself in a towel, ran outside and grabbed her and the gun and brought her back inside. I told her she couldn't kill herself. Larry just walked around in a silent daze. We were all in a daze. It would take time to come to grips with what really happened. Mom called the police, and then we got in touch with some of our good and close friends and in no time our house was filled with loving, caring people."

Always the one on the spot in a crisis, Dick's older sister, Marnell Gray, arrived from Seattle and took over. The first thing she did was to haul her brother's blood-soaked bed to a big old wood panel truck and drove it to the dump. Later she packed away some of his things. He had kept everything, saved every little memorabilia, including his torn pants from the helicopter crash in Texas years before. Steady as always, her presence lent an air of calm to the emotional chaos Gracie and her children experienced.

But true to her own style, Gracie quickly recovered her composure. No one saw her cry. At the memorial service in the Polynesian bar he loved so well, Gracie told her children, 'Don't cry. Your father wouldn't want you to cry, he'd want you to be strong.' None of them did.

❧

With their mother in control, the Stroms did not dwell on their father's death. They just picked themselves up and went to work. There was no time for introspection, no philosophizing about it. That's Gracie!

But the Strom kids hated it when people asked how their father had killed himself. That really bothered them. However, the nosy individual was simple told the truth: "He shot himself."

What else was there to say? That's what happened. Dick's suicide probably helped Gracie's business. People genuinely sympathized with her. They loved her because she was such a strong woman who picked up the pieces and continued to work, determined to make ends meet.

Sally admitted that for a long time before his death, she had hated her father because he frightened her. He was a violent man, mean and ugly when he was drunk. She'd hide in her closet behind her clothes and repeated over and over, 'I wish you were dead. I wish you were dead.' And then he killed himself. She always felt ... guilty.

Years later, through the older Nancy, Sally began to understand her father – who he really was, the circumstances that contributed to his heavy drinking and eventually to taking his own life. Her older sister told her stories of the last days of their Dad's life, as she sat at his knee and listened to him tell the stories over and over, again and again, each time more desperate than the last.

Nancy wrote some time later *Well in the end, Daddy couldn't live with his stories. The intensity of his despair enhanced and distorted by alcohol and tranquilizers finally took its toll. He decided to sit on the end of his bed in his locked bedroom and blow his brains out. I think it was the only way Daddy could erase his nightmares.*

I still miss him, even the stories. My little sister misses the father she never knew. I miss the Dad the war stole from me.

The discovery of Dick's letters to his mother from 1943 to 1952 finally gave Sally closure with her father's death. She read first hand about the challenges of his life and the effect his time in Korea had on this once brave, strong, and proud man. She understood at last that it wasn't her fault he chose not to live.

After the shock of Dick's death wore off a bit, Gracie faced herself. She had no confidence that she could run a business; she had never operated one. Dick had handled every aspect of the day-to-day workings of the restaurant, while Gracie stayed on the sideline taking care of the customers, being the perfect hostess and entertaining them. Dick was brilliant, but had decided to go into the businesses world and not become a Rhodes Scholar, tempting and prestigious as it may have been.

Gracie sighed, turning back the clock. "He taught me how to balance my own checking account. After we were engaged, he insisted we wouldn't get married until I paid off the purchases I had charged on a credit card. He was definitely a professional and had an excellent head for finances."

With those thoughts running around her head, feeling inadequate and insecure to step into her dead husband's shoes, she decided to put the Sea Hag on the market quickly and find a buyer. An interested party showed up but informed Gracie on the day of Dick's wake at Surf Point Inn that they'd had changed their mind and wouldn't buy the Sea Hag. So much for that.

But then another couple appeared on the scene and announced their interest in buying Gracie's place. Papers were drawn up, seller and buyer met. But the man got mad at Gracie's lawyer when both parties were getting ready to sign the papers.

"Boy, look at this contract," Philip, the buyer said," there's no breathing room in here for us at all."

Gracie's lawyer, Paul, an ex-Marine and close friend of Dick's replied. "Well, it's like the crooked card game. It's the only one in town. So that's the way it is.'"

Well! That remark infuriated Philip. He got to his feet and hissed, "We don't want any part of a crooked card game."

Gracie was devastated, because there went her chance to get out of her business. "The attorney had been Dick's best friend. I didn't have sense enough to say anything," she mused, "It is kind of funny in retrospect, because it was true. Ours was the only bar in town other than Surf Point Inn up the road."

That wasn't the end of problems popping up like weeds on the front lawn. On the very day of Dick's funeral services, followed by a sort of continuous wake at the family's home, the restaurant's building's owners called. Tactlessly disregarding the event taking place at Gracie's, they demanded over the telephone, that she buy the building or they would increase the rent of $150 by $350 per month for a total of $500, Unless one or the other happened, they threatened, they would not renew the five-year lease.

Gracie shook her head. "They didn't know we were having a wake. They just said they had heard that my husband had died. That increase in rent would kill us; there were months when we had trouble coming up with $150. That's when I decided I'd better got to the bank and see if they would lend me the money to buy the building." Little did she know that at that moment she had taken the reins of running the Sea Hag firmly into her own hands.

After Philip walked out of Paul's' office, nobody else showed up with an offer to buy the Sea Hag. Gracie wanted to own that building in the worst way, but was doubtful, being a woman, the bank would lend her a dime. Dick had never taken out a loan except for a home purchase. He preferred to make it on his own. But he did always say that if one needed to borrow money from a bank, not ever to talk to a loan officer but to head straight for the president of the bank who has the authority to loan money without consulting anybody.

Gracie took Dick's advise to heart, marched off to the bank and within moments found herself face to face with Al Guard, the president of Lincoln Bank. The latter was a small bank compared to the ones in the big cities. But as far as little Lincoln City was concerned, it was a pretty big bank – the only game in town. Gracie surprised herself how calmly and businesses-like she explained her situation, asking for the money to buy the building that housed the Sea Hag, She was even more surprised when Al Guard said for her to offer the owners $35,000 for the building, not $60,000 for which they had asked. Gracie did not think they would consider the low offer.

Al Guard knew what a hard working, determined woman sat across from his at his desk. He had financed the home Dick and Gracie bought in Depoe Bay several years ago. He leaned back in his chair and with a wide grin on is face explained the strategy.

He said, "Yeah, but we're talking cash. No-hassle cash! You just tell them you'll get them $35,000 cash for the building. They'll take it." He proved to be right.

"I will always be grateful to that man. He must have seen some quality in me that I had not yet discovered, and," she added with great warmth in her voice, "Al Guard got me listed in Who's Who in Business."

After the president of Lincoln Bank lent her the money for the building, Gracie, acknowledging a new sense for business, got bolder and asked how come the people who served on the bank's board were the only ones able to buy stock in the bank.

Al Guard hesitated for the briefest moment then replied that the bank stock was closely held. He then turned to her with yet another surprise. "I'll get you some bank stock," he said But then best of all, she paid for it with a bank loan. Nothing wrong with that! Gracie's business savvy grew by the minute.

Gracie pondered for moment, then with a slightly puzzled look in her clear, blue eyes, she said slowly, "I really didn't stop to think that all of a sudden, not only was I a widow, but I actually owned my own business, held stock in a thriving bank and was responsible for making all the decisions." This coming of age, growing into an active, successful woman in business and learning the ropes on the way, became her. She took on no airs, was the same dimple-faced, warm and people-embracing individual.

Those who dealt with Gracie in personal and business situations not only discovered her unerring sense of fairness but her well-developed stubborn streak. At the time she found herself a widow it was hard for an unmarried woman to have an American Express credit card in her own name. However, American Express was about to meet a most insistent woman who would not take "No" for an answer. Over the course of a year, Gracie's relentless powers of persuasion won out and American Express awarded her the coveted "Green."

Shortly after Dick's death, Gracie had the opportunity to buy a lot and an old house situated behind the Sea Hag. The purchase would give room for expansion and put a stop to the mudslides. She really wanted this piece of property and followed the advice Dick had given her. Don't go to the loan officer at a bank; go to the president. That's what she did.

Before the banker would loan her the money, he wanted to inspect his collateral. He drove up to the old house in his Lincoln Town Car, smoking an expensive cigar. He got out of his car and glanced briefly at the house. Turning to Gracie he said, "You mean they want $5,000 for that dump?"

Gracie was quick to reply, "Mr. Walden, I don't want you to live in it. I just want you to lend me the money to buy it."

Her ploy worked and she got her loan. – Amazing Gracie was emerging, coming into her amazing self. Over the next thirty years she acquired several other properties and watched her investments grow. She had become a lady of means and with the help of yet another banker Gracie attained what she believed to be the pinnacle of her career.

Tom Moore was a long time customer of the Sea Hag. He was also the president of National Security Bank in Newport. One day Tom stopped by the Sea Hag and asked her to join the bank's board of directors. At that time, the thought of a woman on a bank board was just unheard of. National Security Bank was a successful entity and a perpetual member of *Money* magazine's list of top 100 Independent Banks in the United States. This unique invitation made Gracie proud.

Mr. Moore's family and a few well-to-do investors owned the bank and the Moore family controlled the bulk of the stock. When Gracie questioned Mr. Moore about what his board would say about her joining, he replied, "My family owns the bank. The other stockholders will vote the way we ask them to." Gracie knew she was in.

Sometimes at the board meetings the other investors would query Mr. Moore about the interest rates the bank was getting. Gracie jumped right in. She could tell them how much the bank was charging because she was one of the borrowers.

This was about the time Gracie met Paul Schibig, a former IRS Agent turned CPA who would play a large role in her life. Paul became her CPA first, then her friend, trusted confidant, and amateur psychologist. His long and lasting loyalty to Gracie is typical of the strong bonds she builds with good people.

ⷜ

Among her bag of tricks there was one that served her well. Gracie never wallowed in self-pity. She didn't sit around depressed or feeling sorry for herself. Whenever it was a sink-or-swim time in her life, she rose to the occasion and went to work. Whether she knew what she was doing or not, she acted like she knew what she was doing and it worked. Gracie took after her father in that respect, who had taught her well. She had a younger brother who died when she was growing up. After he was buried his memory was not a subject on which her family dwelled. There was work to do on the farm; after all life was for the living.

Al Sax, Gracie's father, traveled from his home in Cashmere, Washington, to attend the wake and funeral services for Dick whom he had admired so much. Al's own life as an orchardist was the example for Gracie growing up and earned her the title in her teens as the "Fastest Apple Packer" in Wenatchee.

Al had married Agnes, the woman who became the center of his life for 57 years. For more than thirty years, Agnes suffered from rheumatic arthritis, the painful condition requiring her husband to stay near her constantly. Al faithfully cared for her in their home, rather than having her spend her last years in a nursing home.

Raising the Sax brood kept Al involved for twenty years. He considered his family his greatest accomplishment along with the good living he always provided. An insurance policy Al acquired while serving in the U.S. Cavalry during World War I provided the down payment for the apple orchard, a purchase most people couldn't afford in those days Having made his living from the earth, he was both an expert and a lover of agriculture. He told his children, "You've got to do what you want, and like what you're doing." He fully believed that independence is the incentive to do what one wants and to work harder.

"When we worked hard, we didn't realize how hard it was," a philosophy Gracie never forgot. Her voice was strong and clear when she spoke again, "You don't bury your heart with the dead, you say your goodbyes and move on. You do whatever you have to do to survive, and you do it happily, without regrets or woe is me," These wise words confirm her inner strength, her courage while declaring her independence. She told her children to keep their chins up; their father was a Marine through and through, would not have wanted it any other way.

❧

With Gracie at the wheel of her business activities, Nancy, Larry and Sally followed in their mother's footsteps and immersed themselves in the demands of each moment. There was no time for leisure, for camping trips, for catching up with each other at the family dinner table or for any other "normal, ordinary" family activities. The kids were raised and grew up at the Sea Hag. Not only was the Sea Hag home for the Strom family, but it was the place to hang your hat for so many of the restaurant's helpers, one of whom waltzed into the Sea Hag and Gracie's life almost 40 years ago and is with her still.

A young woman, Barbara Mason, lived in Portland in those days, worked for Freightliner during the week, and like clockwork, headed for Depoe Bay to tend bar at the Sea Hag over the weekend. She took to the place like duck to water and loved the work, the people and, of course, Gracie. But it wasn't always just laughs. She will always remember the night when a couple of fisherman brought in two of the largest crabs Barb had ever seen. The two crustaceans were lying peacefully on their backs on top of the bar– seemingly lifeless. But when Barb grabbed one to flip it over, the crab, very much alive, shot out a claw, sunk it deeply into one of Barb's fingers, splitting it to the bone.

Gracie turned gray when she saw what happened. Barb was in excruciating pain, blood was running down her arm and spattered all over the bar. The trick to remove the claw was a challenge. To break off the whole leg would only cause the injured crab to clamp down harder and take off the finger. Finally, someone took a metal bar and pried the offending claws apart.

Throughout the ordeal, Barb kept quiet, her face a mask of courage. When she arrived at work the following weekend, Gracie, with a straight face, told her that some friends were waiting for her in the kitchen, Barb nearly passed out when her "friends" turned out to be two more huge, legs-wiggling crabs. The rest of the gang had a good laugh at Barb's expense.

However, the crab attack did not stop Barb from quitting her Portland job, packing her bags, and moving to Depoe Bay to become a full-time bartender. And that was the beginning of a truly great friendship – sometimes a bit stormy. And, there was a reason for that.

Gracie had always verbalized her criticism and reprimands of employees in public. When Barb who by then managed the business, told her boss that it was not a good policy, Gracie took pen in hand and began writing notes. It was often a good way (certainly a better management style) for Gracie to vent her frustrations by writing them out, ripping them up and throwing them away. But the notes weren't all serious. There were a lot of funny ones, words of praise, reminders or a message about something that happened of interest and worth mentioning. The notes went to the bartenders, to waitresses, to cooks and to the busboys, but not to Barb who preferred toes-to-toes and nose-to-nose confrontations with Gracie. The two of them would go round and round bringing their issues out in the open. These sessions were not always pleasant and sometimes ended up by Gracie reminding her manager who signed the paycheck. Serious and heated as these difference-of-opinions battles were, no damage was done to their friendship. In no time their differences were forgotten and life went on – nothing lost.

One of the pages of her notepad landed on the table of a couple dining in the restaurant at a slow night. They had been giving the waitress a hard time, complaining loudly about poor service. At the time they were the only guests at the Sea Hag and had the attention of everyone – including Gracie. The irate couple kept complaining, adding that they had come to the Sea Hag for years, and knew Gracie personally. Spitting venom, they concluded that they would make sure that she would hear about it.

Gracie had enough. She walked up to their table and asked, "Do you know who I am?"

The couple replied with a somewhat puzzled, "No."

Gracie shot out, "Well, I'm Gracie, the one you've known forever. I don't remember you at all, and I don't appreciate you giving Linda a bad time. You are the only table right now, and she has been taking excellent care of you. I heard it all."

The troublesome guests huffed, "Well! This is the worst service we've ever had and we won't come here again."

With the notepad in her hand, Gracie tore off a page, dropped it on the table with her pen. "Good!" she exclaimed, "would you put that in writing, please?"

When the rude couple responded with added fury, Gracie simply told them in no uncertain terms there was no charge for their meals, would they please leave and not come back. Gracie watched the puffed up individuals leave the premises, their anger still visible in the stubborn set of their chins and thrown-back shoulders. Gracie just shook her head – fortunately, this was a rare happening at the Sea Hag.

꧁꧂

Only in the rare quiet times she had for herself, but not dwelling on it, did Gracie reflect on the events leading to Dick's death. She came to the conclusion that those left behind always can find some reason for being unaware of the signs of peril to a close one on the verge of taking his life. There were those endless telephone calls her husband made to his old buddies from World War II and the Korean War. He called his friends and even people with whom he'd had rarely been in touch. With a drink in his hand and close to the bottle, they'd talk for hours, sharing memories, trying to come to peace with themselves. Many of Dick's buddies were feeling as guilty, remorseful and tormented as he was about the part they played in Korea. In World War II they had all been heroes; in Korea they had been the villains.

Gracie confessed that she must have been blind to the severity of Dick's desperate state of mind; she hadn't had a clue.

She was proud of how her children made it through the difficult and trying times and to this day, she has kept the note Sally wrote describing her sister, brother and herself.

"Gracie always taught her kids to treat all the people they met at the Sea Hag as gifts of God. They paid the bills. She also taught us to follow our passions no matter how bizarre they may be."

A close friend of Gracie's described the Strom family with the following loving and honest appraisal.

Nancy Sax-Strom was born at El Toro Naval Air Station in California, with a baseball bat in her hand and a steering wheel attached to her knee. Who drives with hands anyway? She was taught at an early age how to be a team leader and win the game. She had a talent for decorating and loved to travel. She was always ready to play any time of day. Today, she is a physical fitness guru and drives a Harley motorcycle. Nancy's no fool marrying a younger man, a skydiver, for entertainment.

Larry Fancher Strom was born February 28, 1954 in a crash course of wild ideas, and like his mother, never stood still for long. He had a model airplane business in the old book store; worked on becoming a Herb Alpert trumpet player without sound; was the answer to the bonus question of a high school quiz: "Who Stinks?" He did stink from his weeks of cooking crab at his fish market. Defending his sister, he was going to teach Sally's boyfriend a lesson. But when the kid ducked, Larry's fist hit the brick wall. For some reason he wasn't asked to play on Nancy's baseball team. However, he didn't lack for company, he always had an army of buddies around.

Sally Kim Strom, the family's May 13, 1957 addition, was the chubby girl who liked to color, color and color. For a change of pace she would bury the dead kittens from the dozens killed on the highway behind the Sea Hag. It was a ritual of the transition time for these traffic casualties before they were picked up by the heavens. Making her famous mud pies, teaching life's lessons to her stuffed animals and chasing boys were important stages in her development. Today she paints bold and striking portraits of life, has a Masters in Fine Arts degree, and looks with pride at her grown daughter and son.

In other words Gracie and Dick taught their children to find their passions and discover ways to fulfill them. Dick's was flying. Gracie's is her love of people. Today she is a strong influence on her grandchildren, each insisting she is the world's greatest grandma. However, by her own admission, she refuses to let those grandchildren pass her on the go cart track."

Family truckster, 1968

Gracie's International Driver's License, 1972

Gracie with the Tax Axe, 1979

Gracie, the biker babe, 1980

Gracie at work, 1985

Sea Hag ad, 1982

Gracie and Tessa play the bottles. 1988

*Postcard,
Sea Hag,
1988*

The Sea Hag of Depoe Bay

Gracie Plays the Bottles

*Postcard,
Sea Hag,
1995*

*At the
Symphony,
1999*

Gracie and Wolffish,
1998

Gracie, Stan and Sign,
2003

Larry's Weding, 2000

The dancers,
2002

Coast Guard Commendation, 2004

Michael Dane, 2007

Betty Hall Jones, 1985

Gracie and Stan with Darcelle XV, 2005

Chapter 6

With the ownership of the building in which the Sea Hag was located, Gracie felt a sense of proprietorship that was comforting. And though she had taken on the $35,000 loan obligation to her bank, she was determined to double her efforts toward making the restaurant-bar a destination stop that travelers, vacationers and townspeople would enjoy and remember. Her determination became more intense after her husband's death. Gracie was constitutionally unable to allow any emotional blow to change her optimistic view of the world. It wasn't surprising to her three children that within a year or so after Dick was gone that she attracted men who found her charm and enthusiasm exciting.

Now that the authority of their father was missing, Nancy and Sally remembered how they would ask Gracie for permission to make certain decisions and she would reply absentmindedly, "I don't know. Go ask your Dad."

Nancy chuckled when she recalled her mother's response. "She truly said that, because our Dad had been the authoritarian source of wisdom and Mom was a pushover. You could always do whatever you wanted with Mom. So after he died, we had no rules at all; we had none. We were raised just like Sally said. She compared us to Pipi Longstocking, free to do what we liked. Mom let Sally draw on the walls. She let us jump off the banister. She was just a kid with us. She didn't know what to do, because my father had made all the rules. We thought of Mom as our best friend. She was our father and mother."

Both Sally and Nancy agreed that it seemed as though nobody ever decided anything in the family. Things just happened, like Jim Cutler, Gracie's partner in real estate. He came into their lives when two other men named Jim were calling at the house for Gracie.

"It was so funny," Nancy remembered, "because I would ask her, 'Mom what are we supposed to tell this one?'"

"She'd say, 'Well, if Jim calls, tell him I'm here. If the other Jim calls tell him I'm not.' It was a kind of nonchalant – but uncalculated – vagueness that was both humorous and effective and a part of her makeup.

The two girls had to keep those Jims straight and in the process acted more like a parent than Gracie ever did. The Strom kids were delighted when Mom met Jim Cutler, who became her best friend and anchor. They were never more than just good friends, two people who truly trusted one another. This Jim was a dream – steady and comfortable. Gracie and he were together for twenty-five years.

Not surprisingly, Jim Cutler met Gracie at the Sea Hag. He was married at the time, but he wasn't living with his wife. The girls used to call her the Crazy Lady. Every Friday night and for a long time, she telephoned Gracie's house drunk beyond reason. Then she'd call the Sea Hag. She wanted Jim back, but in her muddled state of mind seemed to have forgotten that they hadn't lived together for years – long before Gracie ever met Jim.

Jim Cutler was the one who got Gracie interested in making various real estate investments, all of which turned out to be highly successful. All of a sudden she was a major partner in some valuable properties all due to Jim's "nose" for recognizing a good deal and steering Gracie in the right direction. The woman who had been so unsure about getting a loan from the bank to purchase the Sea Hag building just a few years ago, quickly learned to work with the bank's money to fund her real estate investments.

"Everybody wanted to be like Jim," Gracie said, "because he put together incredible deals. He had the brains and the vision to get his hands on most of the ocean frontage around Depoe Bay. There was only so much land on the ocean side, and nobody could "make" any more.

"He was a real estate genius," Gracie recalled. "He had a lot of smarts, but had little motivation and was not the greatest company around people. He was a gentle and kind person, but he was just not charismatic. It turned out that I was always the face that went out and made the deals. But he was the brains behind our dealings. We became the best of friends. He was a lonely man and when Sally moved to Portland to go to school, Jim moved in and stayed for twenty-seven years."

His influence was powerful on Gracie and gave her the confidence to stretch and grow, to rely on herself, her uncanny wits and unique personality. The shrewd investments she made with his coaching and recommendations were one thing, but his true value lay in his friendship, his loyalty and his ability to make her see the person she really was.

It didn't seem strange to Gracie that Jim slept in a chair in the living room. He had breathing problems and other health issues, was overweight and didn't exercise. He hated to walk and even drove to the Chinese restaurant next door to the house to have drinks. He simply refused to walk anywhere.

Jim Cutler had become her rock. He was always present and didn't really have a life outside of Gracie. He worshiped her; he loved her. He called her his "little petunia." He was brilliant but he didn't have close friends. He had a few acquaintances and it was probably his high intelligence that set him apart. He graduated from college when he was fifteen years old and confided to Gracie once that it was the worst mistake parents could ever make for their child.

He was planning to attend medical school, but everybody treated him like a little baby and never took him seriously, the boy with a brilliant I.Q. who was isolated from the world because of his genius. He came from a family of senators, politicians and thinkers, but he was world-shy, didn't know how to dress or talk to people. Many loved him because he was well read, trustworthy and he was wonderful to Gracie. Every time he turned around he had made another acquisition: there was the mall in Depoe Bay, the post office, a liquor store, a tavern and houses. He got into all those enterprises with great success and Gracie was his partner. The good old Sea Hag had become the cash cow that made it possible for Gracie to invest in Jim Cutler's projects. Jim had a bottomless bag of talents and among them was architectural design. He created and supervised the first thorough remodel of the Sea Hag and did a great job.

Jim became Gracie's hero and was always near. He wasn't the adventurous kind of a man, but he was an avid reader. He'd accompany Gracie on her errands and waited for her in the car reading for hours and hours on end – perfectly comfortable. Although Jim drank quite a bit, he was one of those who believed a person shouldn't drink until the day's work was done. He'd go to the Sea Hag at Happy Hour and stay till closing time. He kept a diary and night after night as he sat at the bar, he wrote down what happened during the day.

Some people who didn't know Gracie's family well insisted it was highly dysfunctional. To this criticism Gracie responded that the only people who are really dysfunctional were the ones who are too damn functional. She raised her family in the era when "dysfunctional" was what people were doing – being dysfunctional.

Sally later compared the situation to a sort of Hugh Heffner/ *Playboy* thing. It was he who'd characterized, "The glorious seventies," when birth control was out and before AIDS showed up. It was a time that will never be again. And so, the happy times rolled on unrestrained.

Back at the Sea Hag, Nancy, who was now managing the bar, hired people to work there. She did a great job finding the right person for each position and saw to it that everybody had fun.

Life with its constant changes, challenges and gifts brought Gracie another interest. She met John Holiday, a logger and a bright and handsome man at the Sea Hag. She and John became great friends. He was fun to be around and made Christmas one year a memorable time for Gracie and her family. And it all took place at the house.

"There was a big Christmas tree," Gracie recalled, "and gifts for everybody heaped under it."

Sad and a bit lost, Nancy didn't come downstairs that Christmas morning to join her family, who had been waiting for her so that they could begin opening presents. As many young people do who had lost a parent, she resented John's presence as though he was the intended replacement for her father. But Nancy didn't really care for John, because she missed her father to whom she had been so close.

Getting impatient, and perhaps wanting to teach Nancy a lesson, John just smiled and told Sally and Larry that they could have her presents. They were jubilant. 'Yeah, this is great!' So they opened all of Nancy's presents, including the top gift, the *White Album* by the Beatles. When Nancy finally appeared downstairs, she was peeved and quite upset when she discovered her Christmas gifts had been turned over to her sister and brother. However, before the day was over, things settled down, everybody laughed a lot, and Nancy ended up getting along just fine with everyone.

John Holiday was close to Larry, taking him out in the woods where they logged together. Larry liked the man. Unfortunately, he lost part of a finger in a logging accident, but that didn't stop him from responding to John Holiday's daily wake-up call. The big logger would appear at Gracie's house at six o'clock in the morning to get him out of bed and head for the woods. "Come on Larry, get up lazy-bones," he'd yell in full voice, and Larry would tumble out of bed, still groggy with sleep as though he'd been up late the night before.

John also had become the self appointed Chief Vermin Hunter in charge of reducing and, better yet, eliminating the unwelcome rat population that sneaked into the Sea Hag. These nasty rodents lived in the rafters underneath the Jimco docks where they snatched fish heads and offal swept from the trawlers' decks. They were great big wharf rats, some as large as a house cat. Grown people shuddered just thinking about those vile, horrible creatures "from hell." One of those gross pests got into the Sea Hag while Gracie was closing up one night and as she went by the service window it jumped out in front of her. "Wow!"

"That's it," she said to herself, a hot warning note in her voice as the offending rodent scampered away. She dropped everything, locked the door and went home. When she told John what happened, he said, "I'm going to kill that thing." She had no inkling he was coming to the Sea Hag the next night with a gun and waited by the freezer for the rat to show up.

Gracie stopped him. "I'm not going to let you blow up the freezer."

Her warning was to no avail, John was ready to get that rat and any of the rodent's relatives that crossed his gunsight. But rats, not unlike their foe the cat, had more than one life. They couldn't get rid of that rat or of the others. All the merchants made war on the ugly, furry beasts, shooting at them in the bay with rifles.

Gracie's eyes looked back remembering John as a great hunter, and highly successful when he went after the rats on the Sea Hag's driveway. He could shoot anything dead within eight feet. But then came the day, when my relatives, Dick's sister and her husband, were due to arrive for a visit. They were just pulling up the driveway behind the restaurant and saw all the rats scurrying about. The unwelcome rodents were running toward the back door of the Sea Hag, but John was there with his pistol. Deadeye John shot them one by one. Then he said to me, 'We've got to bury these vermin before anybody else comes up,' and with that, dug holes in the back parking lot — graves for the dead. My sister-in-law was impressed."

"The rats were truly a plague," Gracie said, "anytime they sniffed food they sneaked in or tried to get in. In those days we offered "All You Could Eat Steamed Clams" to our customers. Needless to say, everybody and his brother came. For five dollars you could stuff yourself on clams until you burst. Five dollars was a lot of money then. But our customers ate until we thought we'd go broke. Every time a guest ordered another bowl of clams, we'd moan, 'Oh my God, we'll never make it.' But we did. Unfortunately," Gracie chuckled, taking a big breath, "the rats, too, loved clams and would raid the garbage to get the empty shells and scrape off vestiges of meat. With their strong, pointed teeth those monsters could easily break clam shells."

Talking about rats, Gracie recalled how John was a big practical joker. She described how one time to scare her, he tied a dead rat on the hallway light cord in the Sea Hag. Since the ceiling was high, a long string hung down to be pulled. John knew Gracie always arrived in the dark to open the Sea Hag or closed up at night. She had to reach up in the dark, search for the string then pulled it down. "I must have screamed like a banshee," she laughed, "because what I grabbed was the dead rat. Its tail was tied to the light cord. I almost jumped out of my skin, but John, of course, thought it was real funny."

Gracie always displayed a marvelous, genuine sense of equanimity and had trust in life's happy endings. According to her daughters, she encouraged them to go wherever they wanted and do whatever they pleased because they'd only be young once. She even suggested they wear sexy clothes. Her philosophy of youth was, "Your body's never going to look as good as it does now, so you should show it off while you have it."

When Gracie learned Sally had been ticketed with an MIP (Minor in Possession) citation, there were no questions, no carrying on about the subject – no guilt, no shame; just good advice á la Gracie. She gave her daughter instructions on how to appeal to the judge. "If you're going to go to court, McMullen will be your judge. He loves to have pretty girls appear before him. He'll go easy on you if you wear a cute, sexy and girly outfit. Don't wear any of your gunnysack dresses. And," Gracie added with a knowing wink, "act innocent."

Sally didn't wear a gunnysack. She showed up in the courtroom in a short, green velvet skirt topped by a sleeveless vest. The carefully selected outfit left little to the imagination.

Sally had been ticketed for drinking beer at a kegger held by the high school kids on the Siletz River near Kernville. She was caught before she could get away and got a summons to appear in court. When Sally faced the judge in the courtroom, the first thing he asked was, "How much did you have to drink? I see you told the officer five or six gallons."

"Well I didn't mean that." Sally said, "I was just kidding."

He said, "Well that isn't anything to kid about. Well, we'll give you five days in jail – to be suspended."

Sally started to cry.

The judge was perplexed. "What are you crying about?"

"I don't want to be suspended," Sally sobbed.

"She didn't know the meaning of the word suspended as in the legal lingo," Gracie explained, "she assumed they were going to hang her, I guess."

∞∞∞

There was no end to Gracie's escapades and her involvement with her city – Depoe Bay. It was about 1970 when she was elected to the Depoe Bay Sewer Board. Her half-hour campaign was the result of a complaint from a visitor who was standing across the street from the Sea Hag. He was fascinated by the ocean waves smashing against the see wall and shooting geysers of water through blowholes. The pressure of the turbulence shot spouts 150 feet high. At times they showered observers with drenching rain.

The man was awed by the spectacle, but changed his mind when he felt something wet slap him in the face. He tore it off and was astonished to see that he held a square of soiled toilet paper in his hand. And when he bent over the sea wall to look at the receding ocean the visitor was assaulted by foul fumes from human excrement. Outraged, he phoned the newspaper in Newport. His complaint made the front page and it was responsible for Gracie's decision to seek election to the local sewer board.

She knew as well as many other merchants in Depoe Bay the source of the toilet paper and the smell rising from the bottom of the sea wall when the wind was right. There was strong opposition to the formation of a sewer district and it led, Gracie learned, to fistfights over differences of opinion on how to solve the problem. Depoe Bay's future depended on a cleanup not only for the sake of not offending visitors but also for the sake of sanitation.

"We did a lot of late night drinking after we closed the bar," Gracie said, shaking her head. A blush of a smile played on her lips as she continued, "And with a lot of that going on, a lot of wild and wooly, world-changing ideas bounced off of the Sea Hag's walls. Just thinking and tossing around ideas of things we could do was fun. We'd got to the subject of the upcoming election for the sewer board, and it was unanimously decided that the two old fellows who had been on the water board since God created the world, needed to have some competition. They had opposed any changes that would replace the ancient raw sewage pipes that poured waste into the sea from businesses that faced the highway and from homes on the hill above that were connected to old septic tanks that leaked downhill into the ocean."

The upshot of the late-night bar discussions was the suggestion: "Why don't we run you, Gracie, for the sewer board?"

"I said a flat No! I'd die if I didn't get elected. So why would I do it?"

They had an answer, Gracie recalled. " Well, we'll do it as a write-in."

The groups around the bar did the most productive thing – they each had another martini while they thought about it. It was Harold Lee, a wise and successful businessman who was the most innovative one. He offered his big black Lincoln Continental convertible for use in Gracie's short campaign.

"We'll take my convertible with the top down," he suggested "and with Gracie in the back seat we'll go all around Depoe Bay. We'll have a megaphone with us, and we'll offer a vote for Gracie is a free drink and a cup of chowder at the Sea Hag. We can cover the whole residential area in half an hour."

Gracie and her Sea Hag crew had fun planning her write-in. All the preparations were accomplished in two days before the election. Gracie instructed everybody how to vote and urged all of her employees not to forget to sign their ballots. On the day Harold Lee and Gracie toured Depoe Bay's residential areas in his black Lincoln Continental convertible, she got on the megaphone and shouted, "Roll up your pants, it's too late to save your shoes! A write-in for Gracie is a free drink at the Sea Hag, and a free cup of chowder."

"I think," she said, "there were less than 200 people around to vote. But we just went up on Schoolhouse Road and made our pitch. Of course it was illegal, but the benefit of proper sewers for the town was worth it. It was sure less illegal than a lot of the politicians who were voting gravestones in national elections. Our brief campaign worked," Gracie said with a note of satisfaction in her voice, "I got more votes than the two old men combined."

New sewers were authorized soon after Gracie became a board member. Bob Jackson, Depoe Bay mayor, put the whole sewer plan together. The first thing he did was to hire an engineer.

"Bob really knew what he was doing," Gracie said. "He told us we had to fund a sewer plan and he found a state law that would not permit us to organize a district, so we put an assessment of two dollars on each property in the town to help pay for the engineer to start his work. Then we applied for state and federal funding of more than half a million dollars."

Gracie's energy and effortless ways of getting into new and different things reflected in so many of her actions and was second nature to her. By working on expanding and securing the success of the Sea Hag, she went far afield and automatically raised public awareness of her town. She put the small fishing village on the map. Alert and interested in everything that came along, she always found a new way to promote her town and the Sea Hag. As mentioned earlier, Depoe Bay was known as the coastal town with the smallest harbor in the world, which was unique, but Gracie used to tell all the people who came by busloads from all over the world, that Depoe Bay was the only place where the migrating whales lingered and could easily be observed. The whales never went north or south; they loved Depoe Bay and stayed right there. She told that story so often that people believed it. So, all of the publications of the Chamber of Commerce advertised the whales' preference for Depoe Bay. The word got around and became gospel because nobody challenged it.

"I sat there and chuckled to myself because I swear on the Bible I made the whole thing up. Visitors believed the same family of whales stayed year after year," Gracie confessed, the impish look in her eyes turned on high.

The other funny thing that happened which really put the Sea Hag on the map was the television show *Real People*. The whole crew arrived to film the seals in the aquarium located at the end of the block from the restaurant. People flocked to see the friendly seals clap their flippers when they were fed food the tourists bought. When the *Real People* crew completed filming the seals, they came to the Sea Hag and shot film of Gracie playing the bottles. Her performance with her musical bottles appeared first when the film was shown on television, followed by the seals clapping. It looked as if they were applauding for her. That was great publicity, the kind one cannot buy.

Gracie's generosity and genuine love for people was evident in everything she did. She fully believed in the reward system. Big or small, her personal attention and favors were memorable. The kids who came with their parents to the Sea Hag thought Gracie was the greatest. She always gave them a prize − little sailor figures carved from wood − if they'd come into the bar and clap when she played the bottles. The youngsters loved her for it and returned to the Sea Hag years later when they were older and could sit at the bar.

The characters that formed the composite tableaux of the Sea Hag were drawn from every strata of America and they became their true selves under the carefree, undirected, free of judgment guidance of Gracie Strom.

There was Glenda, a bartender and a large, pretty girl. She was so embarrassed after she got drunk, took off her clothes and streaked like a naked nymph through the Sea Hag one night, she never showed her face again in the bar.

"Somebody probably dared her to do it," Gracie chortled, her face was one wide, dimpled grin, "she just ran naked through the bar, out the front door, and hid in a station wagon.

"I didn't actually see her streak through he bar," Gracie said, "but I learned about it quickly." She heard about Glenda's performance from a man who told her, "Glenda's hiding in my station wagon and I can't get her out."

"Oh God, she's been out drinking all night," was Gracie's assessment of the situation. With her friend, Joey Gibson, who happened to be at the Sea Hag that night, Gracie took over. The twosome got to the station wagon, and Gracie in her best military "holler" voice ordered Glenda to get out of the car. The girl streaker appeared slowly – naked as a plucked-clean jaybird holding on to the car door for momentary cover. Joey and I grabbed her and rushed her into the Sea Hag. Joey located her discarded clothes and headed for the ladies room. By the time her rescuers had the uncooperative party girl dressed, people were knocking on the door wanting to know if there was a problem.

"No, everything's fine; Glenda's just a little drunk," Gracie assured her friends, "Oh my God, I thought," she remembered. "My heart went out to the poor girl. Even though not many people had seen her in her birthday suit, Glenda believed the whole world was pointing a finger at her. . . shame. . . shame."

A day or so later, when Gracie called on Glenda the embarrassed young women wouldn't answer the door bell, and through the closed door conveyed her intent to Gracie, "I'm going to commit suicide," she cried, "nobody will ever forget."

Gracie begged and cajoled her to come back to work. "It's okay," she tried to calm the hysterical girl, "it's okay! Like anything else, people will have something to gab about for a while, and when they tire of the subject, they go on to other things. Nobody will remember a year from now."

Neither words nor reason changed the disturbed young girl's mind. She moved on down the coast to Coos Bay, where she insisted she would stay.

Another member of Gracie's cast of characters was 93-year old Ernie Kimball. She always took him along when she drove to Portland to buy supplies at United Grocers. Not known to be slow behind the wheel, her heavy foot on the gas pedal caused Ernie some consternation. He never complained, just held on tight during the ride. Upon reaching Depoe Bay, Ernie would sigh with relief. "Made it again, Gracie," he would utter.

Ernie had a terrific sense of humor. He married a woman twenty-five years his senior and mentioned that it was the smartest thing he did. She was a loyal companion and waited on him hand and foot for many years. On her deathbed, peaceful and gentle, the couple held hands. Her last words were, "I love you, Ernie."

Ernie was a true family friend. He even flew to New Mexico with Gracie to attend the wedding when Sally married her first husband, Steve. They stayed in a one-room cabin with only one bed. Ernie told Gracie, "Don't worry. I found an ironing board. We can put it between us."

On those rare occasions when Gracie smoked a cigarette, Ernie used to tease. "It's better to smoke here than in the Hereafter," he quipped, grinning from ear to ear. He was good company, grateful to have a friend like Gracie and be part of her family.

Then there was a lost-at-see tragedy Gracie recalled. A note of sadness veiled her voice when she told the tragic story of a family of four who all worked at the Sea Hag. The mother, Lee, worked at the restaurant, and her husband was the Sea Hag janitor. The couple's son and his fiancé – both barely twenty-one years old – had been given jobs by Gracie as well. Impressed and deeply influenced by the money the fisherman from Ilwaco spent at the bar, the young couple decided to earn some "big bucks" from commercial fishing.

The ocean was rough and rolling the day Rogal and his fiancé, Shelley, went out in the little boat he had borrowed to try their luck fishing for big fish. Rogal had little experience in handling a small vessel and a roaring ocean, and Shelley had never been on a boat. The inevitable happened; the two were lost at sea, their bodies never found. Now their names are engraved on a bell buoy at the Depoe Bay Coast Guard Station, and Rogal's sister Rhonda's painting of a sunset on the ocean gracing a wall at the Sea Hag pays tribute to young lives lost.

Sadly, that was not the end of the family's tragedy. More heartache was in store for Lee and her husband when their surviving son was killed by a hit and run driver. But there was always Depoe Bay's Patron Saint at hand – that sturdy Gracie with her "porch light on" to help heal the wounds of life's tragedies, big or small.

Her philosophy that life is what it is, and that every tragedy is offset by humor was the catalyst that kept her heart strong, her outlook in the pink, full of optimism and, just as unsinkable as the *Unsinkable Molly Brown:* "She ain't done yet."

But when you roll it all up in a bundle, there was always more fun than problems at the Sea Hag, a place all kinds of folk wandered into. Gracie got to know well some of the famous people – including Henry Fonda – who came to the Sea Hag. She greeted the famous with the same familiarity she extended to every customer.

Gracie met Jack Nicholson who was filming the motion picture *One Flew Over the Cuckoo's Nest* at the State Hospital in Wilsonville, Oregon. He came to Depoe Bay on a weekend and headed straight for the Sea Hag. Some one had told him not to miss seeing the smallest harbor on the continent and meeting the bottle-playing hostess of the Sea Hag.

Then there was handsome Paul Newman, filming *Sometimes a Great Notion* at nearby Kernville on the Siletz River, a film about a family-operated tugboat business hauling logs on the river. The location was a natural for the story and the Sea Hag was just as natural for the actors and the crew to relax, drink, eat and meet the curious locals as well as the Sea Hag's enthusiastic, jump-for-joy bottle-playing hostess.

One scene from that motion picture was poignant for Gracie. It was when the veteran actor, Richard Jaekel, Paul Newman's brother in the film, slipped between two logs in the river, went under and drowned. The love of her life, after Dick died – the logger, John Holiday, who had captured her heart, but left her with a deep ache of loss when he died only two years after they met.

Not to be forgotten by many, was the night when a couple from Texas parked their large RV in front of the Sea Hag and walked into the bar. As the evening progressed a lively debate ensued about the pros and cons of owning and traveling in an RV with Gracie and some of her friends crowding around the bar. The hour got late, no one felt any pain and for some unknown reason, the happy group found themselves standing in he middle of Highway 101 serenading the huge visiting RV with their rousing rendition of *The Eyes of Texas Are Upon You* in sync with the ear-breaking honking of the motorhome's horn. Except for the small audience that had gathered, Depoe Bay slept through it all. As it turned out, no one had any recollection if a decision was made whether or not an RV was a good thing. Or did it even matter?

The stream of the Sea Hag's customers was a never-ending source of excitement, adventure and even entertainment. One night in the early 70s, six men entered into the dining room – obviously not locals. They ordered steak and lobster and a good wine; the best of everything. The tab came to today's equivalent of more than $400. Finished with their gourmet meal, the men sneaked out through the back one a time without paying.

Gracie quickly realized what happened. Grabbing her keys and hurrying through the restaurant, she saw the last one getting into a late model car. She jumped in her Caddy, (her first new car) and set off after them. She chased them about three miles north of Depoe Bay to Fogarty Creek State Park. Following them down to parking lot, she blocked the sole exit road with her car.

Fortunately, she had one of the early car phones, placed a call to the police, then jumped out and confronted the six scofflaws and said, "The jig is up!"

She then informed them about her call to the police. She scolded them for running out and demanded they pay her. They were reluctant at first, until she reminded them about the cops on the way. If they paid up, she may let them go before the cops arrived.

The six men, caught for their crime, scrounged around in their billfolds and pants pockets, finally coming up with the money for their expensive meal. They tried several times to get Gracie to settle for less, but she held fast and insisted the tab being paid in full. Once she had the money in her hands, she let them go, admonishing them never to return. She then called the police and told there would be no need to send an officer. She had done her thing. Amazing Gracie!

cๅๅๅ๏

After Jim Cutler passed away, Gracie rented the house next door to hers that Jim had occupied to one of her chefs, an older man with a young male companion. They were quiet tenants, keeping to themselves, often working in the back yard, a small plot of hillside land. With a gift and a touch for interior design, the new renters immediately began remodeling the house and turned a "shack" into a charming and valuable property. He just knew how to "do" things. For Gracie, he picked out the best computer and bought her a fabulous leather briefcase she still has. Of course Gracie paid for the purchases.

One day Gracie and Barbara – the latter was living with her at the big house – were looking out the window and saw FBI agents surrounding the renters' house. Throughout the day agents carried covered pallets out of the house. Gracie and Barb decided they probably weren't bodies, but still didn't know what was going on. Needless to say, they were uneasy and curious.

Late in the day an agent knocked on Gracie's door and explained they had just completed a large marijuana bust and had arrested the occupants.

The next day Gracie and Barb inspected the now empty house, and discovered a trap door in the bedroom that lead to a windowless cellar, a perfect place for a marijuana-growing operation. The growers had been quite sophisticated in the process, and had gone as far as diverting the flow of water from the sloping yard to a collection spot for use on the plants. The women were amazed what had taken place next door, right under their noses – so quietly, so unnoticed. All that crime, in sleepy little Depoe Bay no less. In the end, the older man took the rap for the younger. He had a good lawyer from Eugene and managed to get off with a fine and no jail time.

cๅๅๅ๏

Then there was a steady stream of the regulars who brought fun and laugher to the Sea Hag. Chief Farmer, from the local Coast

Guard station was quite a character in his own right. He used to come into the Sea Hag reeking of aftershave lotion. One evening Gracie asked him "What do you have on?" The erstwhile Chief responded, in front of a full bar, "I have a hard-on but I didn't think you could smell it." The Sea Hag was not a place for the faint of heart.

Among all the great people who worked at the Sea Hag and the many who loved Gracie, there was always one bad apple. One of them was Bill Swanson (not his real name) who was the book-keeper for the restaurant and managed one of Gracie's real estate properties, "Gracie's Landing."

It turned out that the bad apple was a thief. He stole thousands of dollars from his employer. Bill's hand-in-the-till activities were discovered by a new man in Gracie's life. The man was a shrewd, highly experienced businessman with a nose for treachery and a detailed knowledge of construction.

Bill Swanson was a master at manipulation. He was especially effective with electronic transfers of money. By the late nineties, the Sea Hag was one of many enterprises Gracie and Jim Cutler had acquired. As a result there were several bank accounts. The CPA auditing the accounts talked only with Bill about discrepancies he found and never discussed these "irregularities" with Gracie. It was Stan, Gracie's new husband, who became suspicious of some of the invoices and payments. He arranged for a new audit with a different CPA and the truth came out.

Bill had a much younger accomplice/boyfriend who did construction work. Between the two of them, they had worked an embezzlement racket that remained undetected until Stan stepped in and started sniffing in the books. He told Gracie, "You know I'm a builder. I caught some things they were too careless about. That happens when thieves get too sure of themselves."

Casey, the boyfriend, had graduated from Brown, and Bill Swanson was a graduate of Cambridge. Swanson had lived in Germany as a practicing psychologist for the military. Everything he did seemed to be documented. Casey, however had a different kind of documentation, namely a stolen identity. The younger man was really Bill's son, Tracy, living under an assumed name.

Bill always deferred to Gracie, was charming and depend-able, but never, like other employees, got close to any old hands who worked at the Sea Hag. He appeared to be very professional, but remained charmingly aloof – probably because he was protecting his criminal activities. Gracie would invite him for dinner, but for some reason he would never make it. Something always came up to prevent him from accepting invitations. Gracie admitted that if one wanted to con somebody, she was a pushover.

When Stan started looking through all the books, and he found out that the cook was getting paid off by Bill. He had his friends, buddy-buddies of whom he took care – good care. He was writing all kinds of checks for them. In one case, he wrote a check on the business account to bail out a friend who had lost a lot at gambling. He gave the man $30,000 of Gracie's money.

The audit discovered that in one of his transactions, Bill had made a $14,000 electronic transfer out of the "Gracie's Landing" account. Then he bought a cashier's check with the $14,000 from the West Coast Bank Corp. and deposited that check on a Visa bill to a bank in Minnesota. There were other outrageous thefts pointing to the fact that Bill thought he had a forever-good thing going and Gracie was too careless and naive to protect herself against scoundrels.

After Stan got a copy of the cancelled check for the Visa bill in Minnesota, he and Gracie confronted the embezzler and fired him on the spot. His face showed no regret or remorse when he handed over his keys and he walked quickly away without a backward glance. Tracy was arrested under a fugitive warrant after eighteen years on the lam, eventually being charged with five felonies.

Gracie never prosecuted Bill. Hiring lawyers, going to court would be time consuming. She and Stan were well aware that white-collar fraud was not worth pursuing. The jails were full of violent offenders and had little room for con men.

❧

In the thirty years that passed like a ship sailing through storms at sea into peaceful waters, Gracie at the helm of the Sea

Hag surmounted challenges, setbacks, tragedies and triumphs. During that time Gracie and her Sea Hag had earned an ever-growing national reputation as a unique place of good fun, good food, good drinks and a charismatic, charming "hoot" of a hostess. Gracie and the Sea Hag had become a unit of one, like one breath, one heartbeat. Nobody ever referred to just one and not the other. Year after year people returned to the Sea Hag and Gracie. Her circle of friends had widened and reached across the nation, her financial struggles were over. She had become a woman of means, but remained undisturbed and unimpressed by possessions and her life style – never a show-and-tell for all the world to see – is still modest and unassuming. Stuff held no meaning for her. Gracie kept on growing and Depoe Bay grew right along with her.

Regional and local newspapers and magazines tripped over themselves to interview Gracie Strom and the Sea Hag, who has been in print so many times, that she could wallpaper a mansion with the articles and photographs she has accumulated. Nothing Gracie did or was involved in rarely escaped the eager ears and eagle eyes of the news-hungry reporters. The media loved her and never had a bad word to say about her.

She took all the praise, the glory and the tinsel in stride with a shoulder-shrugging, so-what attitude, making light of what others clamor for and wear on their sleeves. When reminded of her achievements, her face dimples and her reply is always the same. " Oh well," she would comment, "I've just been lucky; I've been damn lucky." Most cherished in her accumulation of life's gifts above all, was the gift of fun. And fun she had; some of it walked in, but most of it she brought to the table.

Among the memorable people who came into Gracie's life at the Sea Hag was George Lindeman. He was the local barber with a great love for music and had become a virtuoso on the violin. He had been raised in a wealthy East Coast family, was well educated, with an appreciation for places that were small, tidy and friendly. Lindeman found his niche in Depoe Bay after traveling widely. He had no ambition to be a big frog in a small pond, so when he discovered the town with the smallest harbor in the world and no barbershop, he soon set up shop.

The Sea Hag became one of his favorite places to be and he often brought his violin with him. After one or two warm beers – he didn't like his beverages cold – he always retired to the deck of the Sea Hag facing the ocean. There – minus his pants – standing in his boxer shorts, he played lively and haunting tunes. To the best of her knowledge, Gracie was certain no one ever asked George why he played in his skivvies. Gracie's youngest, Sally, created a large painting of George playing his music into a breathtaking sunset. Taken by the whimsy of the painting on a visit to the Sea Hag, Judy Hoffer, then CEO of Meier and Frank Department Stores, captured by the scene Sally depicted, bought the painting on sight for a respectable price. It was Sally's first large dollar art sale.

Bill Lamb, the Portland supermarket entrepreneur, visited the Sea Hag when he came to stay for weekends at his summer home near Depoe Bay. He had written a small booklet listing the exciting bars in Portland where singles dreaming about finding mates could meet those of the opposite sex. Lamb did not neglect the Sea Hag in his description of places where romances were nourished. Gracie's staff didn't need much encouragement to become matchmakers. It was intriguing and natural for girls in particular to act as icebreakers with simple lines like, "Joan, have you met Sam? He's an engineer. Isn't he cool?" Clary and Jerome, Arlen and Cherie, Lloyd and Barbara, were just a few of the Sea Hag veterans who enjoyed subtly steering young men and women together. Matchmaking was second nature to the folks at the Sea Hag, where ocean waves were transformed into waves of love.

One of Gracie's favorite memories was her invitation to play her whisky bottles as a participant in the Sixth Annual Eugene Symphony Battle of the Batons Contest. Among those performing, Gracie was the most unusual and of course non-traditional musical talent. The Olympic-style competition, sponsored by Northwest Natural Gas, began at eight o'clock in the evening and was held at the Silva Concert Hall of the Hult Center in Eugene and over the years had become quite a prestigious event.

Sharing the stage with Gracie were several other regional restaurateurs, news anchors from Eugene radio and television stations, the President of the University of Oregon, and other Eugene personalities. Judges were chosen from an impressive roster of community leaders and Battle sponsors. The Battle of Batons was the major fund-raising concert of the season for the Eugene Symphony. Sponsors noted that though the fund-raiser wasn't exactly art, it was show biz with familiar music, comedy, costumes, and the unexpected. Gracie recalled her performance with glee for the competition was intense.

"About twenty contestants presented their musical talents," she said. "And we massaged the judges and brought live Dungeness crabs from Depoe Bay. I conducted the 100-plus member, black tuxedo-clad orchestra playing the theme from *The Sting*. Beautiful girls in the twenties-era hats and gowns with cigarette holders paraded on the stage, and there was even a cop in his royal blue uniform with a night-stick on the scene. He interrupted my bottle playing to arrest me for possessing bottles of liquor since it was Prohibition and booze was illegal.

"I retorted, 'Don't you know this collection of bottles is the world's finest musical instrument?'"

"They look like liquor bottles to me," the cop replied.

"That's why you're a cop and I'm a renowned conductor," she replied with authority.

"We received the Bronze Medal for our performance – not bad for an apple knocker from a little town in Washington – not playing the piano, not playing the violin – just bottles," Gracie's eyes danced and her laughter filled the room.

Chapter 7

In the early years of the Sea Hag – as mentioned before – Gracie had drawn attention to her place by performing her singular act of booze-bottle playing. It drew people from all over who heard about the young woman whose enthusiasm was contagious, her hospitality irresistible. Few had her gift of making people as welcomed, comfortable and cared for as the Sea Hag's hostess.

Later on the Sea Hag – offering some variety of entertainment to her customers – hosted popular musicians who came to perform for one month at a time. Among them were Frank Gaither, Rick DiBlassic, Betty Hall Jones – the latter a diminutive woman who was famous for the miniature matchboxes covered with seashells she handed out to customers.

And, in the late eighties Gracie was proud to have Michael Dane play at her place. He was the Hawaiian musician who was informed when he was seven years old that a rare eye disease was destroying his vision and would eventually render him blind for the rest of his life. This sentence to a world of darkness did not discourage Dane. He proved his musical genius by playing with Diana Ross and Ray Charles.

Michael was hired by the owner of Salishan Lodge who heard him perform in Hawaii and asked him on the spot to come to the Oregon Coast. After the Resort at Salishan was sold, Dane played at the Sea Hag making it the place to be. His music-loving customers would dance the Hula Hoop, the Bimbo Stick and My Front Man. A seasoned performer, he knew how to get the attention of the crowds. One of his great entrance leads was, "And, here's Gracie – she gets a lot of requests but she plays anyway." His introduction never failed to elicit chuckles and vigorous applause from a happy audience. Michael and Gracie made a great team. Gracie played the bottles and danced while Michael played her theme song, *The Old Gray Mare She Ain't What She Used To Be*. When the music would stop, Gracie would often tell rhymes she created. Three of her favorites go like this:

One martini is great,
Two at the very most.
Three I'm under the table
Four I'm under the host!

◦⋙◦

Gracie had a little watch,
She swallowed it one day.
The doctor gave her castor oil
to pass the time away.
The castor oil did not work –
The time it would not pass.
Now if you'd like to know the time of day
You can look up Gracie's –
Uncle. He has a watch.

◦⋙◦

Gracie had a little lamb,
She also had a bear.
I've often seen her with her lamb
But never seen her BARE.

❧

Many famous visiting performers may have lent a momentary touch of "Big-Town" atmosphere to the modest Sea Hag, but when it all was said and done, it was Gracie people came to see and they never tired of her foot-stomping, hand-clapping bottle-playing act.

Another Sea Hag character was Gary, a veteran waiter who always took great care of the customers. Four ladies came in one time to have tea and cookies in the afternoon. One wanted sugar in her tea, another one asked for lemon, the third requested cream and the last one insisted that her tea be served in a heated and clean cup. Gary promptly returned to the table with the tea, cookies and four cups. He asked politely which of the four ordered a clean cup.

Joining the ranks of memorable characters that blew on the ocean breeze landing at the Sea Hag was former President Nixon's maitre d' at San Clemente. Julius Szabo, a Hungarian who had managed to escape the Nazis during World War II with guns blazing all around him as he ran for his life. He was later captured by the Gestapo and sent to a German Concentration Camp. Julius' life was saved by General Eisenhower when the general personally inspected some of the horror chambers and opened them to news reporters to broadcast the atrocities of the death camps to the world.

After the war, Julius worked a few months for Eisenhower whose letter of recommendation to the Waldorf Astoria established the Hungarian in the United States. He left behind him his mother, father, sisters and brothers who were victims of the Holocaust. According to Gracie, Julius was a dapper, wonderful fellow, a man of about sixty when she hired him as chef. He had come to Depoe Bay to work at Pantlee's or the Surf Point Inn.

When the glamorous resort burned down and was converted into an RV park, Julius hired on at the Sea Hag.

People loved Julius because of his Continental manners and his suave polish. Customers who had frequented Pantlee's followed him to the Sea Hag. Julius brought a sense of friendly high class to the Sea Hag Sometimes acting as maitre d', his European courtesy and impeccable manners flattered women and they cherished his gesture of kissing their hands. He wore a white tuxedo for special occasions and gave the Sea Hag a glow of sophistication. He was strict with the servers about their decorum and ran the Sea Hag as though it were his own. And he didn't believe in free drinks or extra portions without payment. Julius was with Gracie for years until he met a widow and fell in love. The happy couple was married at the courthouse in Newport. Jim and Gracie stood up for them at the wedding and gave the newlyweds tickets to Budapest to visit the homeland he left years before.

❧

Always a defender of the rights of people who were often ignored by politicians who became autocratic after they were elected to office or came into positions of public power, Gracie was angered in 1979 when Lincoln County property owners were confronted with the indiscriminate boost of property taxes. Everybody in Depoe Bay was furious and it just seemed natural that they called on Gracie Strom to organize a protest.

Gracie was only too glad to head the angry citizens group because the tax assessment on her Sea Hag had been raised by 500 percent. The object of the mass gathering of irate Depoe Bay residents and business owners was to assemble at the Lincoln County Courthouse and demand an explanation and a reduction of the tax hike.

"We got the ball rolling the day before the public demonstration," Gracie recalled. She started by urging her Sea Hag stalwarts to get on the telephone and start calling people. Nancy was there waving her sign that said, 'Roll up your pants – it is too late to save your shoes – Taxpayers." Nancy had never forgotten that original catchy slogan that won her mother's election to the Sewer Board as a write-in candidate about nine years earlier. Jim Cutler made all the signs and put them on wooden sticks. He even sharpened the axe, a lonely leftover from a survival kit Dick and Gracie had purchased in Spokane during the Cuban Missile Crisis. Finished with a sparkling coat of shiny gold paint, the forgotten tool had finally come to some good use. When that was done, Jim wrote *Gracie's Tax Axe* on it in stark, black lettering.

"I shouted at Ross Miller, the tax assessor to come out of his courthouse office: Come on Ross, if you can't stand the heat, get out of the kitchen.

"Before we marched on the courthouse," Gracie continued, "I went down to the Newport Police Department and got a parade or demonstration permit. They had never heard of one and tried to give me the run-around but I insisted. The police chief even wanted to join us by the time I finished with him. Television cameras were on the scene and we had the attention of all the news media. I was interviewed and we had a ball – Nancy loved it, being the introvert like her Mom. Jim just shook his head, but being the sweetie he was, pretended he was busy and he couldn't march in the parade. But when one little old 68-year-old lady screamed as he was standing by our van, 'Come on, join the march. Are you for or against us?' He succumbed to the challenge and joined the parade."

Gracie's taxpayer protest did result in some determined action from the bureaucrats. Friday's march followed closely on the heels of the county commissioners' announcement that they would probably be seeking $400,000 from voters for the county budget. The week before the commissioners had announced that they did not want to ask the taxpayers for additional funds.

The commissioners had already pruned $1 million from the budget, including the $46,000 requested by the Lincoln County Women's Resource Center for operation of their center and shelter house.

Another protest was brewing in Lincoln City, where hotel and motel operators complained that sewer and water bills were up 200 percent to 800 percent from what they had paid the year

before. The protests got the attention of the media and eventually
the attention of the Lincoln County Commissioners, who
rescinded most of the tax increases and made sure to discuss with
the citizenry before raising them again.

Gracie gives credence to the saying that to stand still one
becomes a target. Well, this lady is always on the move; she
doesn't know how to stand still.

❧

Among Gracie's early and dearest friends after the purchase
of the Sea Hag in 1963 was Stan Allyn. He was the owner of
Tradewinds Charters, the skipper and fishing guide for thousands
of tourists who came to Depoe Bay over the years. Stan arrived in
the coastal harbor with his flagship, *Kingfisher* in 1941. Years later,
the two met and it became a friendship that blossomed and lasted
for almost thirty years until he passed away in 1992. In each other
they quickly recognized a kindred, adventurous soul and the
opportunity to develop a beneficial relationship.

Gracie was a true matchmaker and a natural cheering
section. She always recommended to customers who were interested in fishing or whale watching to seek out Stan Allyn. She
handled the referral in such a hush-hush manner – for-your-ears-
only – that the visitor's curiosity was aroused.

"You know," she would say confidentially, "he was the Coast
Guard volunteer and a noncommissioned officer who had a
machine gun mounted on his boat during World War II. He
patrolled the Central Oregon Coast after Pearl Harbor. He was on
the lookout for Japanese ships. Stan knows the waters around here
like the back of his hand."

Gracie's introduction to Stan was always reciprocated by
him when he suggested to his clients that they have a hearty
breakfast at the Sea Hag before going out on the ocean and recommended they take along a lunch that would be prepared for them.
One hand did wash the other, and the visitors to Depoe Bay took
away good memories and glowing reports of fine hospitality and
great fishing.

While Gracie was familiar with some of Allyn's personal history, tourists came to know him best because they admired the beauty and craftsmanship of the *Kingfisher* and the graciousness of its skipper. Designed in 1940 by Allyn, *Kingfisher* was built by Westerlund Boat Works in Portland for $10,000. A solid wooden ship from the keel to the top of the mast, the boat had a hull of prized white Port Orford cedar fastened with bronze screws to bent oak frames. The vessel's trim and brightwork were mahogany, and its cap and rubrails were iron bark. The ship had a large wheelhouse complete with a full galley, four bunks and head facilities. There was a flying bridge on the aft deck, and jutting from the spacious railed foredeck was a pulpit that brought the *Kingfisher's* total length to 52 feet. No doubt, she was a beauty.

The vessel's varnished natural finish was covered over with military gray when Stan Allyn volunteered himself and his boat for military duty after December 7, 1941, just as Gracie had confided. Appointed a Boatswain's Mate First Class and armed with a machine gun, Allyn and the *Kingfisher* patrolled the waters off the Oregon Coast with orders to "radio his position and 'run like hell' if he saw a Japanese submarine."

When the *Kingfisher* was returned to sportfishing, Stan was unable to remove the gray so he painted the boat white and blue with a red trim. Aside from a 25-foot mast and crows' nest, the boat's most distinctive features were the long outrigger poles used for fishing. "Just about every size and type of fish was brought aboard the *Kingfisher*," Gracie said. "The famed charter vessel also was a place for romance where many proposals and weddings happened, and the boat always led the way for Depoe Bay's annual Memorial Day Fleet of Flowers ceremony to commemorate those lost at sea."

"Stan Allyn was a memorable man, and such a good friend, and he was quite a storyteller," Gracie said. "He typed his yarns on an old manual typewriter in his Tradewinds office, banging out a number of magazine articles and several books. One of which was titled, *Heave To! You'll Drown Yourselves*."

On June 26, 1991 the *Kingfisher* celebrated her fiftieth birthday and a short time later was accepted for the National Register of Historic Places. At the end of the boat's career the vessel was donated to the Lincoln County Historical Society to preserve the boat and keep it as part of its collection to document the history of charter fishing on the Central Oregon Coast,

❧❦❧

Gracie, who raised her children in the same nonchalant, freewheeling and generous way she approached all life and everything in it, looks with pride and contentment at her offspring. They all survived the bumps and detours along the road of growing up. All three kids, now middle-aged adults are successful, productive human beings, have been on their own for years.

"Larry opened his own flight service in Lancaster, Ohio in the eighties," she spoke proudly, showing a newspaper clipping of a handsome young man standing beside an airplane. Larry went on to establish a Fixed Base Operation (FBO) in Lancaster, Ohio, fly Lear Jets for the aircraft factory, and started yet another FBO at Fall River Mills, California.

"Sally," she continued, "attended the Cornish School of Art with scholarships to Drake University in Florence, Italy and England. These are all her work," she points out, waving her hand over the wall directly behind the huge sofa in her house on which hang numerous paintings; abstracts, seascapes and idyllic scenes in greens and blues. "She must have inherited her talent from her father's side of the family because I can barely write my name," laughed Gracie.

"Nancy spent three years at the University of Oregon," Gracie reminisced wistfully. "Both girls have lived in Europe, Africa and South America for a while, Sally is the artist and involved in many art-related projects. Nancy is all about physical well being and everything that is connected to it – from exercise to nutrition."

Did she worry about them when they were younger and out from under her wing? No! No! Not Gracie. She protested, "I think you worry about them more when you can see what they're doing. I didn't worry nearly as much when they were away, because I didn't know what was going on. I didn't have any control over what was happening in their lives half-way around the world, so why worry?"

To her children's collection of the countless stories and anecdotes of "Moments with Mom," her grandchildren who adore her and think she's better than cool, now can add their own experiences with their delightfully down-to-earth, and at the same time, deliciously unpredictably eccentric grandmother. And from the tales their mothers tell occasionally, they get a kick out of the story about the time Gracie took her teenage brood to Europe on a sightseeing holiday. In Germany, she bought a hippie-type Volkswagen bus (their motel on wheels) and the four of them traipsed around Europe for weeks. They visited a lot of countries and had a good time until they got sick and tired of each other and of their confined togetherness in a mini bus. Nancy bailed out and saw the rest of Europe on her own, while Gracie, Sally, Larry and the bus returned home.

Recalling her solo European travels, Nancy said, "I was in Italy when I called home, and Mom told me on the phone, that I couldn't come home because she was living vicariously through me. Another time when I called her collect from Egypt, she told the operator she wouldn't accept the changes, but to tell me to call her again when I got closer to home when it would be cheaper."

Looking back, a warm glow of remembrance settled in her eyes, and her voice held back the laughter. "I'll never forget picking up my only Christmas present at the post office when I was living on the island of Ibiza. It weighed a ton and I had to carry it a couple of miles to my place. I kept sweating and putting it down to catch my breath, wondering what she'd sent me that was so heavy. Finally, when I got to my cottage and opened the package, I couldn't believe my eyes. Oh, Mother! She had sent me a case of tuna fish, and here I was – living by the sea where all I ate was fish."

And here Gracie thought it had been such a good idea; after all, fish was her "staple," too.

In her forty-four years at Depoe Bay, Gracie not only became a beloved character to thousands who met her at the Sea Hag, but was a supporter and friend to many of the people who made the coastal town their home. And that included her staff that benefited from her kindness and generosity and who would walk though fire for her. Being under Gracie's umbrella of caring changed the life of many who came to work at the Sea Hag and chose to stay to this day.

Among her friends was Dennis McKenzie, whose filling station sat catty-corner across the street. Dennis helped Gracie and her crew and took care of all their rolling stock, fixed their mechanical problems or got a stalled car going again. He was a patient fellow and most understanding, even when Nancy took out his gas pumps with her car.

She had parked her Triumph Spitfire on Gracie's rather steeply inclined driveway. The next thing Nancy knew, the darn car rolled down the driveway, across Highway 101 and came to rest at Dennis' station after taking out his two gas pumps. Only the newly installed rockery at the edge of his lot kept the Spitfire from rolling 75 feet down into the ocean. Gracie helped out Dennis until he got his pumps reinstalled and operational. Just another day in the life of Gracie.

She became so well known in Depoe Bay and beyond that people were always amused at the different forms of idiosyncrasies that dictated her life. One can never say that Gracie played by the "blue book of the ordinary." She did it her way. One of her children remarked that when Mother got an idea about something, she became so absorbed in what she was doing that she forgot everything else. The whole world would drop away like a sunset dropped into the sea – nothing could distract her and interfere with the matter at hand.

There was an unforgettable moment when Gracie bought a new car, a spit-and-polish, luxurious Cadillac. She was so pleased with the new and shiny automobile because in the past she'd always had crummy old cars. The minute she saw a hint of dirt on her new car, she rushed out to wash it. She grabbed a box of Spic and Span, turned on the hose and started scrubbing vigorously.

Was she dressed for the occasion? Of course not! Standing on her driveway, she was still in her flimsy, silky negligee when she turned on the water to attack the offending spot of dirt. Waving the hose wildly here and there, she got soaked – and nothing, but nothing, was left to the imagination. Did Gracie give it a thought? Of course not. After all, highway traffic below the scene did not stop – it just slowed down to get a better look at another scenic wonder of the Central Oregon Coast.

In the process of running the business by herself, making decisions and watching the flow of money, she had become quite shrewd and penny wise. When she needed to have tile work done in the entryway of the dining room and the bar, she hired a contractor who agreed to lay the tile after 2:30 in the morning when the bar closed. He had to be finished by 5:30 in the morning when the restaurant opened. She wasn't about to lose patrons during the daylight or at Happy Hour. A shot or two of a rich dark liquid in a glass was an extra reward for the tile layer to give him an incentive to get his work done in three hours during a time when everybody else was in bed. He was one happy tile man.

Of her three children, Sally lived closest to Gracie, a few miles away in Newport. One day several years ago Gracie, who was in her late sixties, met with Sally and told her daughter she'd not been feeling well and described a big lump she'd discovered several months ago near her stomach. One doctor had told her it was probably the result of constipation and had given her a prescription.

The lump persisted and finally, she was examined again and learned the lump, the size of a football, was cancerous, but it was contained. She had to have surgery. Gracie was just beside herself. She was told the surgery was dangerous and she might not recover. Angry, she said, "Don't tell me that stupid thing. I'll be scared going in and may die on the operating table."

Her family gathered around quicker than a flock of birds heading south, and stayed at her side in the hospital until the ordeal was over. Typically, Gracie made a lark out of the gathering, and took her people to dinner eat the evening before at Ruth's Chris Steak House in Portland, where everyone always wanted to eat but didn't because it was so expensive. For her group of twelve supporters Gracie rented hotel rooms at the Red Lion Inn next to the hospital.

"Well, old girl," she told herself, "if you're going to die tomorrow … might as well have fun today."

At dinner that evening, Gracie looked around the table at those she loved and he said, "If I die it's okay because all my family is here." And everybody was.

Nancy came to Portland from Bend and slept beside Gracie in her hospital room at Oregon Health Science University. She didn't really sleep; she dozed in a chair. Whenever a problem arose, Nancy was always the one who charged in and took control. She was good at demanding things and telling people what they needed to do. Needless to say, Gracie recovered, the family breathed easier and the Sea Hag's mistress was back in action within three weeks.

Amazing Gracie!

By the age of seventy, most people have slowed down, cutting back on work and reflecting on the past while occupying the proverbial rocking chair. But that was not for Depoe Bay's live wire.

For Gracie in her seventies, work was the good life and she had no intention of disappearing into the sunset off the beautiful Oregon Coast. She sold two of her real estate holdings – Gracie's Landing in Depoe Bay and Gracie's at Smugglers Cove in Newport – and redoubled her efforts and attention where it had all begun forty years ago at the Sea Hag in Depoe Bay.

"You have to do something all the time to keep going and do something useful," said Gracie pointing to her newly remodeled restaurant and bar. "This time, we closed the Sea Hag for three weeks to get it all done." While retaining the Sea Hag's well-known nautical ambiance, like the inside of a ship, she nevertheless overhauled the place back to front.

The old U. S. Coast Guard dinghy/salad bar was replaced by moveable buffet tables. A wait station was changed to open up view windows to bring in the ocean, and lighter, brighter furnishings took the place of old, dark chairs and tables. Not only did the changes give the restaurant and bar an upscale feel, they also made room for eighteen more seats in the dining room. That alone, Gracie smiled in her mischievous way, makes the cash register ring. And Gracie was not happy until she posted the Coast Guard wall with photos of the men and women who have served in Depoe Bay and Newport, past and present.

"Everyone loved that," Gracie said. "People come back years later to show the photo gallery to their families."

Of all the changes that happened with the Sea Hag along the years, one thing has not been altered and that's Gracie's engaging personality – and her bottle-playing talent – which have made her a legend in her own time. The gimmick she wanted to have in order to attract business and make the Sea Hag stand out in a crowd of restaurants along Highway101 took on a life of its own and fulfilled her wildest dreams.

Gracie and her bottles have become a kind of honkytonk thing, some serious music lovers might venture to say. Her own mother, Gracie admitted, would have had a fit. What? With all those years of expensive piano lessons, that girl is playing what? Heaven forbid! However, not even music snobs or wretched souls who are watching Gracie make foot-tapping music, dancing her bar spoons over a gallery of whisky bottles, can resist getting into it, clapping along enthusiastically. So much for Beethoven, Bach, or Brahms.

After forty-three years in business Gracie is indebted to the people, her workers, who like Nellie Munson became more like family. Several of the employees, including Bobbie Lane and Bonnie Chavez, are still working at the Sea Hag today with the same dedication and enthusiasm they had from day one. Gracie also credited the long-time manager, Barbara Mason, and in-house talent, Michael Dane, for contributing to her continued success.

"Everyone has been so loyal. These great people make their home and raise their families here. I've watched them all grow up; now they have their own children. They are my world," said Gracie, a soft note of awe in her voice. "And," she added, looking out of the huge living room windows straight at the blue Pacific, "A world of give and take, of gratitude and a hell of a lot of fun."

All serious thoughts erased from her face, Gracie laughed out loud, blue eyes sparkling and cheeks dimpling. "Life is good," she sighed happily.

Several years ago, her crew surprised Gracie by compiling a cookbook of famous Sea Hag recipes. Displayed at the checkout counter at the entrance of the restaurant, the little book has sold several thousand copies. Always thinking of doing something nice for her, Gracie's girls created a wall-mounted display case full of clippings about their famous boss. Without attending lectures, without taking copious notes at leadership seminars and without a degree in psychology — just doing what comes naturally — Gracie created a uniquely balanced relationship with her Sea Hag family, and applied the same philosophy in dealing with the community. No one could have chosen a more fitting name for her. Grace. It fits like a glove, like a second skin; Grace ... spelled G r a c i e.

Soon, death interfered with life once again. Not long after her surgery, Jim Cutler died. His death was a loss that wounded her with an overwhelming grief. Cutler was the man who had devoted a quarter century of his life to Gracie, a patient, caring, gentle man whose personal attention to her was like an unwritten love letter. By his actions, his thoughtfulness — his anticipation of her unspoken needs and desires always foremost on his mind — he demonstrated an affection and loyalty that never wavered. Gracie was the woman whose responsibility he had chosen to bear with a grace and appreciation that outdistanced common words of love or the transient physical clinging. He was her knight in shining armor who demanded nothing more of her than to be steadfast and happy in her presence.

When he fell desperately ill and the emergency flight helicopter flew in from Portland to take him to St. Vincent's Hospital, Gracie followed his ambulance to the small airport in Newport where he transferred to the aircraft. Several cars had formed a small motorcade behind her — cars filled with those who admired Jim Cutler and wished to be present when he left them. The younger ones, who climbed upon the roof of Gracie's Cadillac to catch a last glimpse of Cutler being lifted into the helicopter, were choked with emotion. Here was a dear friend leaving – perhaps never to return. It was a sad moment to be long remembered.

For Gracie who knew in her heart that she would never see Jim alive again, it was a crushing, devastating and empty feeling. Jim's death a few days later was a big blow in her life. It was a piercing stab of grief, for it was the culmination of the sorrows she had repressed in her heart when Dick Strom took his life, when John Holiday died, and when her father passed on. Jim's death, after twenty-seven years of her close companionship with him, was a loss that staggered her as it magnified her previous losses and left her in a solitary well of loneliness.

But life distances itself from death like a long night gives way to a new day. New experiences introduced into her life acted like a bridge that helped Gracie recover from her grieving. New challenges renewed her brash obstinacy that always surfaced when she knew something was wrong. It was in the late nineties that Gracie accused the Depoe Bay Chamber of Commerce of acting stupidly to solve the need for public toilets for visitors. Her criticism reminded some old timers of her brief and one and only political campaign to be elected to the Sewer Board and its success thirty years earlier.

Calling the city's solution to new toilets for downtown "a disgrace," Gracie Strom – in no uncertain terms – let the city fathers know she wanted the outhouses out of her parking lot.

The portable toilets installed by the City of Depoe Bay behind the Sea Hag were to accommodate the public while restrooms were to be constructed as part of a new shop-office complex.

"They're smelly and an eyesore," said Gracie, who never minced words, and was familiar with the frustration dealing with bureaucracy. "How does it look for people from out of town to have to use an outhouse? This is a disgrace!"

Earlier, under pressure from businesses and the Chamber of Commerce, the city had placed the toilets on the parking lot it leased from Gracie for $1 per year. The restroom shortage was apparent when desperate visitors were directed to a nearby leather shop or the Aquarium Gift Store down the street and across the highway, then to climb up the stairs to a restroom. A year earlier the city struck an agreement with John Woodmark on public restrooms. The deal was for Mr. Woodmark to build them, and the city to lease them.

But some members of the City Council thought Mr. Woodmark broke the deal by changing the mix of retail shops and offices he planned to open smack dab in the middle of downtown. The change, they said affected the parking code and as a result they wanted the builder to produce three more parking spots before the new restrooms may be opened.

"We've gotten to our limit with him," said Ron Newark, a councilman who was seeking reelection. "We gave him exemptions for the restrooms and the breezeway, but we can't exempt the parking."

Finally, Gracie erupted with scorching indignation. Rick Beasley of the *Depoe Bay Beacon* reported it this way: "Businesses like mine and the Spouting Horn serve as primary public toilets for the throngs of summer visitors. We've had to spend more than $15,000 a year providing restrooms, not just to our customers but to the general public. The problem with public officials is that they are too wrapped up in their own importance and forget that there's not a municipality in Oregon that hasn't planned for its infrastructure, except Depoe Bay. That's deplorable."

When the mucky dust of argument had settled, when the bureaucratic windbags had run out of air and reason and all had their say, the inevitable happened: modern and clean restrooms awaited Depoe Bay visitors.

"Whenever Gracie has her fingers in the pie," Barbara from the Sea Hag commented, "you can bet your last dollar that things get done. She just makes them happen."

It was in 1980 when Gracie met Norm and Phyllis Johnson. A close and lasting friendship developed between them. Without a doubt, the Johnsons occupied the top spot on Gracie's "Heart List" of favorite people. The couple owned the quaint Sea Town Shopping Center in next-door Newport where they lived until they bought a large three-story bay-front house in Depoe Bay. Two stories of the house sat below street level and Gracie, arriving at the top level above, would pound on one of the windows, bellowing, "I know you're in there hiding from me. Open up!.. Let me in!"

For hours at a time, Gracie would hang out with the Johnsons, often ignoring the frantic telephone calls from the Sea Hag, asking her to get behind the bar and play those bottles. "The natives are restless," one of the callers informed her, shouting her request in an effort to get above the rollicking background noise of the Sea Hag's crowded bar. Sometimes an hour and more would go by before Gracie finally took off to make her rollicking music for her anxiously waiting fans. Keeping track of hours, having a concept of time was not to be found in her satchel of life requirements and important goals. Time to her was simply an indeterminate factor, fluid and flexible.

Usually on Sundays Gracie attended Mass, after which she'd get on her bike and pedal over to the Johnson's place. Can't you just see her, still dressed in her best go-to-meetin' clothes, a string of pearls around her neck and a pair of her trademark gold tennis shoes on her feet dodging in and out of crowded weekend traffic on busy Highway 101? Of course you can. That's Gracie!

From the day she was born, Gracie truly moved within a charmed circle that protected her, supported her and provided happy endings for her that played out again and again. After the Johnson's had completed a series of real estate dealings, i.e. selling some of their holdings, and in order to minimize capital gain tax obligations they were looking for a (1031) Exchange Property. During that period, around the year 2000, Gracie – in a hush-hush manner – had been talking to her close friends about selling the Sea Hag. She made a lot of noise about being tired, wanting to retire. Responding to Norm's suggestion of listing her place with a business broker, she went ahead with it.

By then, the Johnsons' time was running out to find a suitable (1031) property, and half in jest Norm suggested buying the Sea Hag. It turned out that the jest became serious business, Gracie was pleased and so the process of selling her restaurant and bar began. Among the requirements Gracie had to meet, was the taking of inventory. Gracie did not want her staff to know that she was selling her/their Sea Hag. This led to some interesting contortions, as in taking inventory after the place closed and when no one was around. Unfortunately, the plot backfired. Long-time Sea Hag employee, Barbara Mason, spotted the lights on at the closed restaurant and raced over to see what was going on. She confronted the man doing his job, who told her to see Gracie. Well, the cat was out of the bag, and when the Johnson's arrived on the scene several days later, they found the staff in tears, a grey-faced Gracie who hadn't slept for five days and an atmosphere that wreaked of chaos, sadness and confusion. Something did not feel right, and with the transaction almost complete and the papers ready to sign, the Johnsons headed for Gracie's house for a talk.

Bouncing the ball back and forth with a tearful Gracie, and after what seemed an endless discussion, the Johnson's finally told their good friend that they would let her out of the deal – no hard feelings. Gracie protested vigorously that she couldn't do that to them, and kept on tearing up. The Johnsons were as good as the best debaters and eventually convinced Gracie to accept their offer and keep the Sea Hag. They assured her that it would not leave a smidgen of resentment on their long and beautiful friendship.

All's well that ends well. The friends parted with hugs and kisses, a few tiny tears and with their friendship intact. The Johnson's would find another property and Gracie kept the Sea Hag – for a while at least. The time just wasn't right . . . yet.

Life being what it is pulls all kinds of surprises out of its magic hat and often at the oddest times. Man plans and God laughs, as a wise one once said. Here she was, a successful businesswoman in her seventies, loved and admired by family and friends and safe in her charmed circle. Gracie's cup was full. And then it happened; Life had another gift for her. Gracie met a man, fell in love and got married.

Working out at the YMCA in Newport several times a week, she met Stan McDonald, who came to exercise as regular as clockwork. It didn't take Gracie very long to realize that she had found a gem of a man and promptly fell in love. Not waiting around or testing the waters, she jumped right in and asked the man out for dinner. The two went out a few times and together discovered they were a hit.

"I wasn't about to wait around," Gracie smiled, her face a picture of bliss. "There was a bunch of little old ladies at the Y who had their eyes on him," she added, "and I had to work fast."

She may not have known Stan long, but she knew her heart and trusted her impulses — not that she would ever label herself 'impulsive. Someone described her as a "small tank with angel wings flattening objections when they got in her way."

Barbara Mason and Gracie were still doing things together on their days off when Barb asked Gracie what they were going to do on a particular day. Gracie said, "I don't know. I met this man named Stan down at the YMCA and he's asked me to go to dinner with him. I think I'm going to do that."

After about four dates later, Gracie casually announced to Barb, "I want to marry him. I'm going to marry him."

Taken aback and recovering her breath, Barb replied, "But Gracie, you just met him." Gracie responded, "I don't care. He's wonderful. I'm going to marry him." Barb asked Gracie when she was going to get to meet Stan. "Oh, you'll meet him; he's really, really nice," was the reassuring reply and the two kept seeing each other.

Gracie and Stan had gone to Bend to visit Nancy. When it came time to go to bed, Nancy directed each to their respective rooms after sternly telling the couple, "No sleeping together in our house if you're not married."

Gracie lay awake most of the night and thought "He hasn't asked me to marry him yet." It was a long and restless night for her.

The next morning she went downstairs for breakfast where Stan and all of Nancy's family had already gathered at the table. Gracie went up to Stan, dropped down on one knee and asked, "Stan, will you marry me?"

Trying to keep a serious expression on his face, Stan of course replied, "I would love to. I was going to ask you anyway. We will have a ring and a date so we can sleep together."

Gracie's timing couldn't have been better, because Stan, a widower who had made his home at the Oregon Coast for some time, was all packed and ready to move to Arizona to be near his daughter. The happy man, dazzled by Gracie's tactics and recognizing what a grand lady he had met, succumbed to her irresistible charm.

When she broke the news to daughter Sally, she couldn't refrain from joking, "I've decided to get married," she announced, "but don't worry, I'm not pregnant."

Sally was quite surprised, because her mother had known Stan for such a short time. On one hand, she knew her mother's quick-to-take-charge ways, but on the other hand, when it came to men and marriage, Gracie had avoided the wedding vows for years and years. Wonders never cease when it comes to unpredictable, amazing Gracie.

Counting his blessings, Stan unpacked his belongings, moved into her house and proved to be a wonderful companion. Neat and tidy, he cleaned every cupboard she had, every drawer, put every piece of paper in a file. He cleaned her whole house, organized everything and knows where everything is. And more important than that, he loved Gracie and she's madly in love with him.

Shortly after their engagement the happy couple flew to Arizona for a while. Returning home, Sally met her mother and Stan at the Portland airport. Unlike her usual way when Gracie insisted on taking the wheel, she turned to Sally asking her to drive the car back to Depoe Bay. The lovebirds wanted some time to themselves.

"I never drive with my mother," Sally said, "I don't even drive my own car with my mother because she doesn't like how I drive, i.e. I don't drive fast enough and I don't pass the cars quickly enough, and on and on. I got behind the wheel, Mom and Stan sat in the back seat close together whispering like teenagers. There I was," Sally continued, giggling herself silly, "driving her huge Cadillac through rainy, stormy weather with the besotted couple in the backseat kissing, with Dr. Laura on the radio talking about romance and sex. What a setting!"

Stan and Gracie set the date. They were to be married on July 27, 2002, the same day she had married Dick Strom. "Not only that," Sally mused still chuckling, "fate or coincident – she met both her husbands at the YMCA."

The process of getting the wedding invitations out was pure Gracie. She called Barb one day and told her friend she was terribly busy in Newport and would Barb please help Stan assemble all the invitations. Barb did so and when they finished their task, Barb called Gracie and told her she could come home now, to which Gracie replied, "Good. I'm on my way." How well the two women knew each other.

When it was time to address the envelopes, the situation was a ditto to the first task. Gracie was busy in Newport and would Barb please help Stan address all the envelopes. Once again with the job completed, Barb called Gracie and told her she could come home now. Gracie replied with an enthusiastic, "Goody! Goody!" and drove up the hill from the street below her house. She'd been sitting at the foot of her driveway waiting for the call. Gracie was always great at passing the buck on small, tedious stuff and always got away with it. But she never shirked the big demands which life required of her.

The big day finally arrived. At rehearsal the night before the wedding Gracie asked Barb how to walk down the aisle. Barb said she would walk to the music, matching her pace to that of the music. Gracie announced she was going to walk like they did at graduation, imitating the walk done to *Pomp and Circumstance*. This was a harbinger of things to come.

The sun was out full force against a bright, clear summer sky and the Pacific Ocean shimmered in a rich deep blue the day Gracie and Stan got married. Needless to say, the wedding was quite an event and was true to everything that was Gracie – every inch of her. The affair was afreewheeling, loosely constructed and waiting to happen – free flowing, unconventional and a barrel of fun, all of which started at the very beginning.

The church was packed to the rafters with family, friends and the rest of Depoe Bay citizens. Just before the service started, Father Mel Stead, Father Zack, and Pastor Mitch Watney (Stan's minister) appeared. Father Mel addressed the wedding guests. Keeping a straight face and squaring his shoulders he said, "I've been asked to make a special announcement and here it is: *The seafood is so fresh the ocean hasn't missed it yet.*"

Was that ever effective! Gracie's Sea Hag slogan brought down the house — or the church in this case — and set the tone for the rest of the event. Organ music filled the church, Gracie looked radiant as she walked down the aisle to join the waiting wedding party. Unpredictable as only Gracie can be, the crowd watched in stunned silence as the bride broke away, crossed over to a large statue of the Virgin Mary. Standing in front of the Holy Mother's image, Gracie raised her bridal bouquet and shook at her, as if to say, "You and me, Babe!" The crowd recovered quickly from their surprise and took it all in good humor, as did the priests. After all, Gracie was no ordinary bride and this was no ordinary wedding.

She finally made it to the front of the church and the ceremony proceeded normally. When Father Mel got to the part of the ceremony where he asked "Who gives this woman to be wed?"

Larry quickly replied, "My sisters and I gladly give her away and we don't want her back. She's yours; you keep her now." More chuckles, more giggles and outright laughter greeted that announcement.

Gracie and Stan had been fitted for rings six weeks or so before. Barb had been keeping them in the safe at the Sea Hag. It came time in the ceremony for the exchange of vows and rings. Gracie said hers and Stan slipped the ring on her finger. Stan said his vows and Gracie tried to put on his ring, only to discover to her horror that his finger had swollen a little and the ring would not fit. She tried to get it on to no avail. Suddenly, she muttered under her breath "God give me the strength to get this ring on!" And miraculously the ring slipped right on. The power of Gracie's faith showed up again. Amazing Gracie!

Without further incident, the priest blessed the union, the groom kissed he bride, the newlyweds walked down the aisle to roof-shaking applause, and greeted their guests at a grand and joyous reception that ended up to be something between a small county fair, a family reunion and talent show. It was an unrivaled affair at Depoe Bay. Invited or not, everyone was welcome and a happy crowd soaked up the joy and happiness that radiated from Gracie and Stan.

The reception was like a movie star party. Held at the Inn at Otter Crest, it was a great event. There was singing and dancing, all manner of performers including of all things African fertility dancers. People were chatting in groups sipping champagne, kids clutching their cans of soda. Huge platters of fresh seafood and trays of tempting tidbits abounded. The master of ceremony for the party was Darcelle XV, the famous female impersonator from Portland. Darcelle and Gracie had been friends for years. Darcelle, dressed in full-length glitter and sparkle, set the tone for the party. Just after the show started, he was about to make a rather ribald comment when he stopped to utter, "Uh, oh! Daytime. Minors. Forget that!" Uproarious laughter followed and the show was on.

Throughout the festivities, Stan and Gracie stayed at each others side, visiting with their guests, holding hands, blissfully happy. The following week the *Depoe Bay Beacon* featured the hand-holding Gracie and Stan sitting in their new porch swing for two – a surprise gift from the Sea Hag's adoring staff.

After the reception, Gracie, Stan, Barb and some others were gathered around the fireplace talking. The honeymoon had been postponed until the first two weeks in December, the time the Sea Hag traditionally shut down. Barb asked them where they were going to go. "Hawaii", Gracie replied, "Stan's never been there."

Barb proceeded to extol the virtues of Hawaii, telling Stan all the things they could do and how beautiful it was. After a few minutes, Gracie looked at Stan and said, "So, should I tell her?"

Stan replied, "Sure, go ahead."

Gracie proceeded to tell Barb they're so glad she liked Hawaii "Because your tickets arrive tomorrow and you're going with us." Surprised and a little shocked, Barb managed a weak and teary, "Okay."

The threesome had a great time on Maui. Some of the best adventures resulted from exploring the island. Stan was doing the driving and Gracie handling the maps. Barb sat in the back seat laughing. Gracie is "directionally challenged" and kept getting them lost. Barb finally got to the point that she nicknamed him *Turnaround-Stan* because Gracie kept telling him, "Turn around, Stan."

Somehow, they got lost and ended up in one little town and had a terrible time getting out. After asking numerous locals how to get out of town and not having much success, Barb commented, "Ever feel like a rat in a maze?" Peals of laughter followed. With new directions for Stan, the newlyweds and Barb eventually made their way out of the little town and arrived safely at their hotel.

The three travelers had taken turns fixing breakfast during their stay in Hawaii. One day when it was Barb's turn, she decided to fix French toast. There was no syrup in the condo, which was a good reason for everyone to go shopping. The shopping trip got a little out of hand and they arrived back at the condo with new clothes, assorted shoes, and all manner of other stuff, including the syrup. When they were ready to use the syrup the next morning, it was nowhere to be found. It finally turned up days later when they were cleaning out the rented car before turning it in. Barb stuck it in her suitcase. She was on a different flight from Stan and Gracie and got home long before they did.

Back in Depoe Bay, she went to Gracie's house and left the items from her luggage that were the overflow of Gracie's possessions. She stuck a note on the bottle that announced, "Once I was lost, but now I am found," and left the wayward purchase on the kitchen counter.

Barb's phone rang the next night about 11:30 and all she could hear on the other end was a riot of laughter. Mrs. Butterworth's with the note attached had cracked up Stan and Gracie who managed to catch her breath long enough to say, "What a great ending to a great vacation."

The following summer, the "Three Musketeers" – as the threesome referred to themselves – were attending the Lincoln County Fair when they encountered Lars Larsen, a popular radio personality they knew from KXL Radio in Portland. He asked if they were going to be around the following day. If so, he would like to interview Gracie about an article that had just appeared about her in The Oregonian. Gracie told him they didn't plan to come back.

The next day, they were listening to Larsen's radio show when he asked his question for the day, "Should a woman ask a man to marry her?" Gracie heard this and instead of calling the show, she and Stan jumped in the car and took off for the County Fair. Larsen welcomed her into the booth, handed her a microphone and a set of headphones and put her on the air. Gracie, of course, took over the show, turning it into a running ad for the Sea Hag. Barb was listening to this while driving and was laughing so hard she had to pull over and stop the car.

When the host finally got control of his show again, he asked Gracie where they had gone on their honeymoon. She told him, "Hawaii. We took my best friend Barb along and we had a ball."

"You took someone else along on your honeymoon?" Lars asked. "Yes," Gracie replied. "It's because of Stan. He's man enough for two women."

Chapter 8

Gracie's spacious old house on the hillside above Highway 101, with its huge living room windows looking straight down to the bay and framing magnificent sunsets, never had happier tenants. A sharp businessman and organizer, fair and reliable in his relationship with people, Stan took over some of Gracie's responsibilities, which she was only too glad to relinquish. Stan was indeed the man for all seasons – something Gracie's unerring female intuition had known the first time she laid eyes on him.

The Sea Hag and her bottle-playing hostess had been a legend for years by then. People talked about Depoe Bay, Gracie Strom and the Sea Hag in one breath. All her life, Gracie had taken her success in stride, loved her work, but at the same time she was beginning to toss the idea of selling the Sea Hag around again and was getting almost comfortable about it. Who would be the new owner? Who could she trust with the well being of her "child?"

Well, it so happened that the new owner of the Sea Hag had been on the scene for nine years working side by side with Gracie, and like her idol, making the restaurant and Depoe Bay her home.

About 1996, Clary Grant was the new face at the Sea Hag waiting tables. This young woman who closely resembled Gracie when she was about Clary's age, in her thirties, was destined to become the new owner of the Sea Hag. It didn't happen over night, but after almost ten years as a waitress and moving up to the demanding position of operations manager, Clary would become the owner. Her husband, Jerome, described Clary as a woman similar to Gracie in her enthusiasm, determination, and appreciation of humor to smooth the way to friendship.

Jerome, a fisherman, vividly remembered the dark and blustery spring night in April of 1996 when the wind blew him and his partner, Steve Stanson, into Gracie's Sea Hag where the two men took the corner seats on one side of the dining room.

This was the second year Jerome had come to Depoe Bay to work in a little known commercial fishery – harvesting sea urchin along the reefs and rocky shores of Oregon. Using special picking tools, rakes, ring-nets, inflatable float bags and special dive gear, the fishermen carefully pulled these creatures Jacques Cousteau called the "most dangerous animal in the sea" off the ocean floor. The highly prized contents of their shells consisted of five pieces of meat. Packed fresh in little wooden trays, these urchins known as *Uni* in Japanese are auctioned off daily in Tokyo – the largest fish market in the world.

When Jerome tumbled into Gracie's that night, he noticed the young woman waiting on customers across the room. One look at the poised, dark-haired beauty – he fell head over heals in love on the spot. He kept returning to the Sea Hag always getting a table in Clary's section, never summoning the courage to introduce himself, but always looking for a way to break the ice. Finally, one day, as he was standing at the counter on his way out, Clary made her entrance sporting a new curly hairdo. He finally took the bull by the horns and gulped, "Nice do."

He had already told Gracie that he was going to marry that girl. Gracie was quick to reply. "You and every other man in here. What makes you different?"

"Because I'm going to take her to Paris on our honeymoon," he quipped.

Clary smiled at him graciously, a conversation developed, which in turn led to the first date, followed by more dates and in less than a month culminated into a marriage proposal. His luck held and Clary said "Yes."

Shortly after Clary had accepted Jerome's proposal, she asked Gracie for a leave of absence. When Gracie asked why, Clary told her boss she was going to marry Jerome and they were going to Paris on their honeymoon. Another promise made true, another match made at the Sea Hag.

Having worked in her mother's small restaurant at one time, the young woman loved her job at the Sea Hag. For some unknown and mysterious reason, Gracie had kept a close eye on her. When the bar manager position opened up and Clary let her boss know quickly that she was interested Gracie immediately promoted her. The young woman took to her new job like a bird to the air. Satisfied with her managing ability and the way she handled herself with the public and the Sea Hag crew, Gracie promoted her to operations manager.

In 2005 Clary became aware that Gracie was ready to sell the business. After lengthy discussions about the possibilities of owning the famous Sea Hag – a dizzy, head-spinning idea and a towering responsibility – Jerome and Clary decided to take a stab at it. Getting financing for this purchase could be a hurdle too big to overcome. But try, they would.

A bit surprised when approached by the couple's intentions of buying her out, yet recognizing an inner knowing that her interest in the young woman had not just been a casual one, Clary became Gracie's hand-picked successor. Content that she was the right choice, Gracie's mind was at ease and letting go of what had been her life became less painful as the days went by.

The process of qualifying for financing was detailed, time consuming and more often than not – downright frustrating. However, with steady Stan at her side, Gracie's patience stretched like a rubber band, and after months of dealing with attorneys and bankers, almost a year later, Clary was the new owner of the old Sea Hag.

Gracie may have been a hard act to follow, but somehow Clary (the new Gracie) stepped into her shoes with comfort, After all, she had learned about the restaurant business from the bottom up. She had been taught by a master of hospitality, the bottle-playing expert who loved the world and who also happened to be a shrewd business woman. Gracie's spirit will always stay within the walls of the Sea Hag, not usurping Clary's presence, but supporting it.

⌘

And Gracie? Well, when the final vestiges of the separation blues that accompanied the sale of her Sea Hag had left with the outgoing tide, she was as busy as ever. There was time to be with Stan, enjoy an occasional trip, visit with her children and grand-children, play bridge regularly and see her friends more often. People remain her passion and they still flock blissfully into her charmed circle in which she moves with grace and has her being. More than welcome in that circle was Stan's family.

⌘

Gracie never sits still though. Her current project is getting a dialysis machine for the hospital in Newport, Oregon, where she and Stan have built a new house. She regularly plays bridge and treats her extended family to breakfast every week. Her new great-granddaughter, Bella, lives nearby, adding still more energy to Gracie's already full-blown energetic circle.

If she were to take the time to look back on her life, she could do so with pride — the kind of pride that celebrates accomplish-ments and fondly, gratefully embraces those who have been at her side, lending a hand, cheering her on. Ageless as the sea, Gracie still sports that blue-eyed, dimpled, and ready-for-anything look, eager to meet whatever life has waiting for her. Whatever that may be, she can handle it.

She credits her longevity to good genes, the help and love of her children, and her faith. "The children were always there working right alongside me. I couldn't have done it without them," Gracie said recently. Her God has guided her along the way, with help from many of His gifts and messengers over the years.

As far as the home scene is concerned, needless to say, her marriage couldn't be happier. Stan, the ideal companion, keeps their affairs in order, watches over his wife and the two of them will live happily ever after. Gracie still doesn't do much cooking, not even in her state-of-the-art kitchen at her new home on Newport Bay, but then there is always the Sea Hag with its good food, warm atmosphere and the charming hostess, who welcomes her guests with a resounding, "What took you so long to get here?"

And the magic works.

Chapter 9

When the bar and restaurant are humming with the sounds of happy customers and the Sea Hag's staff are turning summer-saults to accommodate the demands of hungry and thirsty crowds, Gracie is at her best. When she is not playing the bottles in the bar to rousing, foot-stomping, hand-clapping applause, she is making her way through the tables, stopping to chat with people, welcoming newcomers at the door and making that cash register ring. One curious thing though happens several times during dining and drinking hours: Customers would leave their tables to go "powder their noses." Often – especially newcomers to the estab-lishment – would be gone so long that concerned friends made their way to restrooms. Entering the narrow back hall, the search party would come to a screeching halt, discovering the lost persons studying the walls of afloor-to-ceiling display of large frames of photos and newspaper clippings, all documenting Gracie and her Sea Hag's amazing history and their modest claim to fame.

One of the earliest newspaper reports was on Gracie's first political action when she ran for the Sewer Committee position, followed by the frequent appearances at local community meetings including the Fire Board, City Counsel, Chamber of Commerce, among countless others.

The *Depoe Bay Beacon* reported that in April, 1979, Gracie got a parade permit and organized a march on the Lincoln City Courthouse to protest a new assessment of property values that represented a 200 to 500 percent increase over the previous assessment five years earlier. She was photographed carrying a small golden hatchet bearing the words *Gracie's Tax Axe*. Her protest march was joined by dozens of people of all ages.

In 1981-82 *Travel Oregon* magazine featured an article describing Gracie as "… more than a woman, she is an event." The same article praised the weekly seafood buffet at the Sea Hag as "… .so bountiful that if you try everything offered … you won't walk, you'll waddle out."

The popular and widely-read magazine *Readers Digest* noted a Sea Hag want ad for dishwashers, referring to them as "Ceramic Engineers".

A reporter covered Gracie competing in the 1992-93 season of the Eugene Symphony Orchestra's "Battle of the Batons – a fund-raising performance featured guest conductor, Gracie Strom. She directed the orchestra while playing the bottles.

In 1993 she received a United States Coast Guard public service commendation for her "dedication and noteworthy contributions" to the Coast Guard in return for their efforts on behalf of the community and the tourists. She had launched fund raising efforts for the Coasties, and often fed the local Guard members and their families."

Also displayed are just a few of the personal letters that frequently arrive at the Sea Hag praising the wonderful food and the delightful experience of visiting with Gracie.

December, 1994 the *Newport News-Times* reported and photographed Gracie's role as Master of Ceremonies for the annual Christmas Tree Lighting Ceremony. And in 1996 Gracie joined a list of celebrated Oregon restaurateurs in the "Hall of Fame" for her many years of service to the restaurant industry.

She has a wall of memorabilia at the Sea Hag lined with

awards with which she has been honored, including Who's Who in America in Business and Finance, the Astra Award for Outstanding Woman in Business, and her First Citizen of Depoe Bay plaque. One can also see a 2001 Grand Sweepstakes Float Award for the Sea Hag's entry in the 2001 VFW Loyalty Day Parade.

In 2001, Gracie was the winner of the Best Local Success Story Award from the *Newport News Times* and was named Queen of the annual Wooden Boat Show and Crab Feed which also honored the 50th anniversary celebration of the Depoe Bay harbor expansion project which took place in 1951. In November of that year, along with the Mayor of Newport, Gracie cut the ribbon at the opening of the new family and youth center at the YMCA of Yaquina Bay – the completion of a project that had her whole-hearted support.

The January 2002 *Salem Statesman Journal* featured an article about Gracie, praising her reputation for kindness and her talent for playing the bottles.

The Sea Hag was frequently the host of celebrities including Hollywood stars Jack Nicholson, Paul Newman and Henry Fonda. Nicholson was a "regular" during the filming of the motion picture, *One Few Over the Cuckoo's Nest*.

In May 2002 Gracie was nominated by the *Depoe Bay Beacon* as Woman of the Year. Some time later – aware of her July wedding – the *Beacon* got wind of Gracie and Stan's upcoming Midday Wedding Shower given by her faithful staff at the Sea Hag. Johnny-on-the-spot, the *Beacon* covered the event, The article mentioned that "The central coast's leading ladies turned out in huge number to fete Gracie and Stan." In spite of the "No-Gift" reminders, some guests refused to arrive empty handed and brought gifts of flowers. The Sea Hag staff, especially, paid no attention to the no-gift request and gave the happy couple a two-seater porch glider for their post-nuptial enjoyment."

A July 2003 Portland's major newspaper in its *Sunday Oregonian Living Section* wrote extensively of Gracie's many contributions to the coastal community and the colorful history of the Sea Hag. In 2004, Gracie was the graduation speaker for the Oregon Coast Community College, duly noted and photographed by the media. And this is only part of all the media attention for Gracie Strom and her place. The Sea Hag staff who put the displays on the walls of the back hall have simply run out of space.

The walls of the Sea Hag's "Back Hall of Fame" are constantly viewed and some of the framed articles read word for word by guests on their way to and from the well appointed powder rooms, often causing a minor traffic jam. And those rescue parties looking for lost diners contribute to the traffic problem, blocking the passage way, remaining rooted to the floor, their eyes glued to the great shots of Gracie, Depoe Bay, the harbor and the stories accompanying them.

One interesting document is not displayed on the "Back Hall of Fame" but is a short note Gracie treasures and keeps safe in her collection of memorabilia.

The brief note reads as follows:

1/19/83
To Gracie:
Close to 50 years ago my father E.C. Segar, the creator of *Popeye*, created a comic strip character by the name of the Sea Hag. I don't know if you remember her or were around then. She was an interesting person. If I remember correctly she started out as an adversary of Popeye then became a bluff, and a strong friend.

I may have some sketches of her in the making. If they will reproduce well, I will send some to you.

Enjoyed your breakfast – excellent.
Tom Segar

❧

Gracie appreciated the media attention and recognition she received over the years, but handled it all with her usual dimpled, eyes-twinkling, unassuming ways that endeared her to all who know her. Now, with Stan at her side, the charmed circle of her life keeps widening, embracing the goodness of life.

That's Gracie!

To order additional copies of:

To get an autographed copy,
please send $20 to:

Amazing Gracie Book
PO Box 80013
Portland, OR 97219

Phone Orders: 541-361-5039

or visit
www.amazinggraciebook.com
where you can order a book and
see Gracie play the bottles!